S. Hrg. 113–668

UNITED STATES STRATEGY TO DEFEAT THE ISLAMIC STATE IN IRAQ AND THE LEVANT

HEARING

BEFORE THE

COMMITTEE ON FOREIGN RELATIONS UNITED STATES SENATE

ONE HUNDRED THIRTEENTH CONGRESS

SECOND SESSION

SEPTEMBER 17, 2014

Printed for the use of the Committee on Foreign Relations

Available via the World Wide Web: http://www.gpo.gov/fdsys/

U.S. GOVERNMENT PUBLISHING OFFICE

95–102 PDF   WASHINGTON : 2015

For sale by the Superintendent of Documents, U.S. Government Publishing Office
Internet: bookstore.gpo.gov   Phone: toll free (866) 512–1800; DC area (202) 512–1800
Fax: (202) 512–2104   Mail: Stop IDCC, Washington, DC 20402–0001

(II)

CONTENTS

ADDITIONAL MATERIAL SUBMITTED FOR THE RECORD

UNITED STATES STRATEGY TO DEFEAT THE ISLAMIC STATE IN IRAQ AND THE LEVANT

WEDNESDAY, SEPTEMBER 17, 2014

U.S. SENATE,
COMMITTEE ON FOREIGN RELATIONS,
Washington, DC.

The committee met, pursuant to notice, at 2:38 p.m., in room SH–216, Hart Senate Office Building, Hon. Robert Menendez (chairman of the committee) presiding.

Present: Senators Menendez, Boxer, Cardin, Shaheen, Coons, Durbin, Udall, Murphy, Kaine, Markey, Corker, Risch, Rubio, Johnson, Flake, McCain, Barrasso, and Paul.

OPENING STATEMENT OF HON. ROBERT MENENDEZ, U.S. SENATOR FROM NEW JERSEY

The CHAIRMAN. The committee will come to order.

[Disturbance in hearing room.]

The CHAIRMAN. The committee will come to order. Mr. Secretary, you have a warm welcome. Having just returned from a coalition-building mission that will determine the breadth of support and course of the anti-ISIL strategy in the near and long term, you are here at a critical moment for the Iraqi and Syrian people, for the region, and for the United States and the world.

Let me say at the outset, in my view, the coalition you are working hard to build will require fully engaged and fully contributing senior partners, a coalition that must be defined not by words, but by deeds. The United States can lead this coalition, but our partners, particularly Sunni partners, must be all in. And I fully acknowledge that getting skin in the game will be different for different coalition partners, but Congress cannot be providing a blank check for the anti-ISIL campaign.

I am pleased by the willingness of our partners in the Middle East to support, fund, and provide resources for this campaign. From Riyadh to Abu Dhabi, from Cairo to Amman to Beirut, our partners are sending the signal to ISIL that they are not welcome, that they have a bankrupt religious ideology, and that they will be aggressively confronted.

Above all, the problems in Iraq and Syria that created an environment susceptible to ISIL's advance can only be solved locally. In Iraq, this means an inclusive government with a national agenda and leaders ready to empower the Iraqi Security Forces and Kurdish Peshmerga forces to take the fight to ISIL.

In Syria, it means training and equipping a vetted Syrian opposition force that shares our vision for a pluralistic free Syria, free of ISIL and all violent extremist groups, but also free of Assad and his regime backers. This fighting force should be prepared to support a post Assad political structure whatever the circumstances under which he ultimately leaves Syria, by a negotiated settlement or other means.

The President has laid out a comprehensive, holistic strategy that purports to integrate all the tools of U.S. power to defeat ISIL. What I expect to hear today are some specifics—the timeline for this mission, the scope, the resources in personnel, funds, intelligence, military assets, and assistance, as well as the role our coalition partners will play. We must be clear-eyed about the risks before providing our enduring support for this operation.

The fact is we are living in 2014, not 2003. We must not repeat the mistakes of the past, given the nature of the threat we face. This means clearly defining the objectives, the political end state that we seek through this anti-ISIL campaign. I want to hear what success looks like in Iraq and Syria, across the region, and what conditions will indicate when it is time to end military action.

Now this is what we know about ISIL: It has brutally, mercilessly, barbarically followed through on its threats to kill American hostages James Foley and Steven Sotloff. It beheaded British aid worker David Haines on Saturday and threatens to execute another British citizen, Alan Henning.

It promotes genocide against anyone who does not share its warped version of Islam—moderate Sunnis, Shias, Christians, Yazidis, minorities. It enslaves women and children. It has seized United States and Iraqi military equipment, has built a formidable fighting force. It is pumping oil and selling it to the tune of $1 million a day to fund its brutal tactics, along with kidnappings, theft or extortion, and external support.

It is recruiting disciples for its unholy war at a frightening pace from Europe, the United States, and anywhere they can find disaffected people. These foreign fighters are crossing often from Turkey, which either because of fear or maybe ideology has declined to participate to stop that flow of fighters and to counter ISIL.

It has declared the territory it occupies a caliphate with intent to seize more territory from United States partners and allies from Jordan to Saudi Arabia to Lebanon. The risk to Jordanian and Lebanese stability is real. It is urgent, and it is grave. We would be fools not to take this threat seriously. ISIL is an enemy of the United States and the civilized world.

Now as I have said many times, temporary and targeted airstrikes in Iraq and Syria fall under the President's powers as Commander in Chief, but if the military campaign lasts for an extended period of time, which I gather it will, it is my belief that Congress will need to approve an ISIL-specific authorization for the use of military force. I am personally not comfortable with reliance on either the 2001 AUMF that relies on a thin theory that ISIL is associated with al-Qaeda and certainly not on the 2002 Iraq AUMF, which relied on misinformation.

I expect the administration, today and in the days ahead, to brief this committee on its comprehensive strategy and the operational objectives by which we will defeat ISIL so we can draft an appropriate AUMF to address the very grave ISIL threat we face.

Now let me be clear. I support the President's strategy and his sense of urgency, and I commend you, Mr. Secretary, for your efforts with allies in the region who also face violent and destabilizing threats from ISIL. Let us not, however, make the 9/11 mistake of rushing into an AUMF—an authorization for the use of military force—that has become the overriding authorization for the last 13 years, has been used for indefinite duration, and has been used from South Asia to the Persian Gulf to Africa and Southeast Asia.

The fact is we need to ensure that whatever authorization for the use of military force we consider is comprehensive and appropriate in scope and duration to meet the threat and sustain the fight. It is our responsibility to answer three fundamental questions. What will it ultimately take to degrade and destroy ISIL? How does this fight end? And what end state do we seek in the region?

We need to get it right, in my view, not just get it fast. And in doing so, we need a bipartisan approach that puts politics aside and the Nation first. This is a long-term effort, and we in Congress must be very deliberate in our consideration of any new strategy, new authorities, and new funding that it will take to meet the new threat we face.

I believe we need to defeat ISIL before they develop the operational capacity to perform a September 11-like attack. I never want to lose as many citizens from my home State of New Jersey or from the United States as we did on that day. That is our responsibility, and it is our solemn obligation.

With that, let me turn to the ranking member, Senator Corker, for his comments.

OPENING STATEMENT OF HON. BOB CORKER, U.S. SENATOR FROM TENNESSEE

Senator CORKER. Well, thank you, Mr. Chairman. And I appreciate the full and broad opening comments that you made and the way you have expressed many of our concerns regarding ISIL and their capacity over time to harm Americans.

I know we are here a few days after the President publicly addressed this, as the Nation and many others around the Western world are—around the civilized world are outraged over the conduct of ISIL, and I know that Americans are greatly concerned about, over time, the effects they might have on this Nation, as you just expressed.

We are also here exactly 1 year and 2 weeks after, in this very room, this committee voted out an authorization for the use of force in Syria. It was one of the bright moments, in my opinion, of this committee. Not necessarily because of the product, but because we all worked together in such a way to come to an end that we thought was best for the country, much in the light and in the tone that the chairman just laid out.

So I just want to start by welcoming our Secretary. We have had some conversations. I appreciate his hard work. But I do want to say, as I have said to him personally, I am very disappointed that the administration has chosen to go about what they are doing without explicitly seeking the authorization of Congress.

I think that is a huge mistake. I realize that part of that, unfortunately, has to do with the political season that we are in, which is, to me, very unfortunate that that might be a factor to some. I also realize that part of the strategy and plan or big parts of it are still being created. And therefore, it is being put together as we move along, and we are really not in a place right now for Congress to fully ascertain what the plan might be.

And as the chairman just mentioned, he is going to deal with an authorization. Our committee will deal with an authorization. But I just want to say to our Secretary, I hope that when that is done, it is done with the administration explicitly seeking that, not saying if Congress wants to play a constructive role, it can and it would be welcomed. But one where you seek it and you lay out in detail for us, in both classified and open settings, what it is we are seeking to achieve and how we are going to go about it.

And again, I know much of this is being made up as we go along. I do hope that the Secretary today will outline the true nature of the threat. I know he was in a meeting prior to coming in here where some of that was being discussed. But I hope that clearly today you will lay out what you think the true nature of the threat is.

Thirdly, and just one glaring piece, I know that Secretaries of State probably do not have the same opportunity that Senators do to visit people in refugee camps and to see people that we said we would support and do not. We have been pushing, in this committee, for years or for a long time to arm and train the vetted moderate opposition. We passed that out of this committee a year and a half ago almost on a 15–3 vote. We have been pushing for it for longer than that.

And in spite of the fact that there are some alleged activities that are occurring, we have not done the things that we said we would do. As a matter of fact, I would say that the position that the administration has taken over this last year and 2 weeks since we were here meeting about the authorization and passing one has led to many of the problems that we are facing today, many of the problems that are causing civilization itself to be fearful.

And again, though, I appreciate the fact that the Secretary is here today, that the administration has stepped forward and has the beginnings of a thought process as to how to address it.

I do want to say that what I have heard about dealing with the moderate opposition to me is odd. I know that the administration, especially at the White House, has stated how generally feckless—to use a word I think that describes it—they believe this moderate opposition to be. And yet we look at this, and today, it is our entire ground game.

I have supported the training and arming of these rebels for some time. I will say I was shocked yesterday to hear that in the Armed Services testimony these rebels are actually going to be used against ISIS. All of them that I have met with, and things may have changed, but their focus has been taking out Assad.

I know they have had a two-front battle or war raging as they have tried to do that. But I am surprised that the administration is basing their entire ground game on a group of people that, candidly, are going to receive very little training under the small authorization that has been put forth, and that that is our entire ground game, which brings me back to point two, talking about the very nature of the threat.

It seems to me the administration has placed many, many caveats on what we will not do, and at the same time, the rhetoric describing the threat is far greater than it seems to me than the plan that is being put together.

And I will close with this. I know that typically when you have a coalition, you have the coalition put together before you announce it. I know in this case, we are announcing a coalition, and we are attempting to put it together.

And I hope that what we are going to end up with is more than a group of coat holders. I hope that we are going to have people who are really going to be doing things on the ground that matter. But I do hope the Secretary, through his hard work, has generated commitments that will matter as it relates to this.

This effort, we all know, is not going to be a 1- or 2-year effort. It is going to be a multiyear effort. Some people are saying a decade. Some people are saying a decade.

And so, I do think it is important, as our chairman laid out, that all of us fully understand what we are undertaking, fully understand the nature of the threat, fully understand the commitment of this administration to deal with this threat in the appropriate way. So I welcome you here today. I look forward to your testimony and to our questions.

The CHAIRMAN. With that, Mr. Secretary, we welcome you back to the committee you so ably and distinguishedly chaired. We thank you for your service to our country.

We know that you just recently arrived from building this coalition, and we appreciate you being here today in order to inform members of what has been achieved, what is in front of us. And with that, the floor is yours.

STATEMENT OF HON. JOHN F. KERRY, SECRETARY OF STATE, U.S. DEPARTMENT OF STATE, WASHINGTON, DC

Secretary KERRY. Well, Chairman Menendez, Ranking Member Corker, and members of the committee, my friends and former colleagues, I really thank you for holding this hearing on an issue that is obviously fraught with all the high stakes that both the chairman and the ranking member have just described and all the members of the committee understand deeply.

And I really look forward to this opportunity to both define the threat that ISIL does pose, the ways in which it does, and, of course, our strategy for defeating it. And all of that could not be more critical for the country.

During the years that I had the privilege of serving here and working with different administrations, it always struck me that American foreign policy works best and is strongest when there is a genuine discussion, a dialogue, a vetting of ideas back and forth, really a serious discussion, much more than an articulation of one set of ideas and then another, and they just oppose each other and they sit out there and there is no real effort to have a meeting of the minds.

So I want to make sure that by the time we are done here today, I have heard from you. I know what you are thinking. And you have heard from me, and you know what we are thinking, what the administration is thinking. And that you have a clearer understanding of what it is that we have done so far, of how we see this, and how, hopefully, we can come to see it together, what we are doing now, and where we go next.

And I state unequivocally, and it is not a passing sentence, that I welcome the input, need the input of this committee because it is together that we are going to be much stronger and much more effective in guaranteeing the success of this effort. And it is a big effort in a lot of ways. It is about ISIL in the immediacy, but as we will, I think, discuss today, it is about a lot more than that.

So I want to underscore at the start, you know, there are some debates of the past 30 years, 29 of which I was privileged to serve in the Senate, that undoubtedly will fill up books and documentaries for a long time, and Iraq is certainly one of them. Iraq has caused some of the most heated debates and deepest divisions of the past decade, a series of difficult issues and difficult choices about which people can honestly disagree.

But I did not come here today and I hope we do not have to rehash those debates. The issue that confronts us today is one on which we all ought to be able to agree. ISIL must be defeated, period. End of story. And collectively, we are all going to be measured by how we carry out this mission.

You know, as I came in here, obviously, we had some folks who spoke out, and I would start by saying that I understand dissent. I have lived it. That is how I first testified in front of this committee in 1971. I spent 2 years protesting a policy. So I respect the right of Code Pink to protest and to use that right.

But you know what? I also know something about Code Pink. Code Pink was started by a woman and women who were opposed to war, but who also thought that the Government's job was to take care of people and to give them health care and education and good jobs.

And if that is what you believe in, and I believe it is, then you ought to care about fighting ISIL. Because ISIL is killing and raping and mutilating women. And they believe women should not have an education. They sell off girls to be sex slaves to jihadists.

There is no negotiation with ISIL. There is nothing to negotiate. And they are not offering anyone health care of any kind. They are not offering education of any kind for a whole philosophy or idea or cult, whatever you want to call it, that, frankly, comes out of the Stone Age.

They are cold-blooded killers marauding across the Middle East, making a mockery of a peaceful religion. And that is precisely why we are building a coalition to try to stop them from denying the women and the girls and the people of Iraq the very future that they yearn for. And frankly, Code Pink and a lot of other people need to stop and think about how you stop them and deal with that. So I——

[Disturbance in hearing room.]

Secretary KERRY [continuing]. It is important for people to understand, there is no invasion. The invasion was ISIL into Iraq. The invasion is foreign fighters into Syria. That is the invasion, and it is destructive to every possibility of building a state in that region.

So even in a region that is virtually defined by division, and every member of this committee understands the degree to which these divisions are deep in that region. Leaders who have viewed the last 11 years very differently have all come together for this cause. They may agree on very little in general, but they are more unified on this subject than anything that I have seen them unified on in my career.

So as President Obama described last week when he spoke directly to the American people, we do have a clear strategy to degrade, defeat, and destroy ISIL, and it is not in its infancy. It has been well thought through and carefully articulated and now is being built in these coalition efforts that began with the meeting in Jeddah and moved to Paris and will move to the United Nations this week when I chair a U.N. Security Council meeting on Friday.

The United States will not go it alone. That has been a fundamental principle on which President Obama has sought to organize this effort, and that is why we are building a coalition, a global coalition. There are more than 50 countries that already have agreed or are now doing something. Not every country will decide that their role is to have some kind of military engagement, but every country can do something. And we will show exactly what that means.

And as I traveled around the region and Europe in the last days, the question that foreign leaders were asking me was not whether they should join the coalition, but how they can help. We are also—and I emphasize this—we are not starting from scratch. This is an effort that we have been building over time, both on our own and with the help of our international partners.

Even before President Obama delivered his speech last week, nearly 40 countries had joined in contributing to the effort to strengthen the capacity of Iraq to be able to strengthen its military, to train, to provide humanitarian assistance. We have been focused on ISIL since its inception as the successor to Al Qaeda of Iraq in 2013.

And back in January, realizing that, we ramped up our assistance to the Iraqi Security Forces, increasing our intelligence, surveillance, reconnaissance, or ISR, the flights that get a better picture of the battlefield. We expedited weapons like the Hellfire missiles for the Iraqis in order to bring their capacity to bear in this fight.

Early this summer, the ISIL threat accelerated when it effectively erased the Iraq-Syria border and the Mosul Dam fell. The President acted immediately, deliberately and decisively: We further surged the ISR missions immediately; we set up joint operation centers in Baghdad and Erbil immediately; and our Special Forces conducted a very detailed, in-depth assessment of Iraqi Security Forces and Kurdish Forces.

We did that purposefully without jumping, as some people wanted us to, because we wanted to understand what is the capacity of the Iraqi Army to fight? How many brigades, having seen what happened in Mosul, are still prepared to engage? Are we getting into something that, in fact, we do not have the answers to with respect to who can do what?

And to date, we have launched—we have supported those Iraqi Security Forces that, by the way, helped in the liberating of Amirli, helped in the freedom of Sinjar Mountain, helped in taking back the Mosul Dam. And now we have launched more than 150 air-strikes, and it is because of the platforms that we put in place last January and even before that those strikes have been among the most precise strikes that we have ever taken.

The percentage, I will not go into it here, but I will tell you, you would be astonished if you heard openly now the accuracy of those efforts. Those were put in place back in June, and those strikes have been extremely effective in breaking the sieges that I de-scribed and beginning to move confidence back into the Iraqi mili-tary.

The judgment and assessments of our military that went over there to look at the Iraqi military came back with a judgment of a sufficient number of brigades capable of and ready to fight. And with the reconstitution of the military in a way that can bring the country together and not be divided along sectarian lines or viewed to be the army of one individual, it is entirely likely that there will be much greater and more rapid progress.

That has given us time to put in place the two pillars of a com-prehensive strategy against ISIL: First, an inclusive Iraqi Govern-ment, which was essential—there would be no capacity for success here if we had not been able to see the Iraqi Government come to-gether—and second, the broad international coalition so the United States is not alone.

We redoubled our efforts, frankly, to help move the Iraqi political process forward, and we were very clear-eyed about the fact that the strategy of ISIL would only succeed if we had a strong, inclu-sive government, and frankly, that required transformation in the government, which the Iraqis themselves effected. With our sup-port and several weeks of very complex negotiations, President Masum nominated Haider al-Abadi to serve as Prime Minister. And shortly thereafter, Prime Minister al-Abadi, again with our support and others, was able to form his Cabinet and present it to the Parliament, and last week, that government was approved.

I have to tell you, it was quite astonishing to be in Jeddah the other day with the Saudis, Emiratis, the Bahrainis, the Jor-danians, the Qataris, the Turks, the Lebanese, and Iraqis. Iraqis in Saudi Arabia, and everybody here in this committee knows what that relationship has been like for the last years.

And to hear the Foreign Minister of Saudi Arabia, who chaired the meeting, Saud al-Faisal, say that they were prepared to open an immediate embassy in Baghdad. That is transformative. The re-sult is something also for Iraq that has never seen before in its his-tory, an election deemed credible by the United Nations, followed by a peaceful transition of power without any United States troops on the ground.

I must say I was sort of struck. Yesterday, the Wall Street Jour-nal had an article talking about Arab divide, but above the Arab divide language is the Shia foreign minister of Iraq, the Kurd president of Iraq, and the Sunni foreign minister of Saudi Arabia, all in communication and jointly working as never before. So I think people need to focus on what has been accomplished here.

As you know, I went to Iraq last week. I traveled. I met with the leaders of Iraq. And throughout the entire process, we have been in touch with regional leaders to ensure that the new and inclusive government is going to receive support from the region.

With this inclusive government in place, it is time for a defensive strategy that we and our international partners have pursued to get things together, get the inclusive government, know exactly where we are going, to now transition to an offensive strategy, one that harnesses the capabilities of the entire world to eliminate the ISIL threat once and for all.

President Obama outlined this strategy in detail. I am not going to go through it in that detail, but I will just quickly say—I will be quick in walking through it. At its core, our strategy is centered on a global coalition that will collaborate closely across a number of specific areas, including direct and indirect military support.

Military assistance can come in a range of forms, from training and equipping to logistics and airlift, and countries from inside and outside of our region are already right now providing that support in these venues. I have also no doubt whatsoever that we will have the capabilities and the resources we need to succeed militarily. And President Obama made clear that we would be expanding the military campaign to take on ISIL in Iraq, in Syria, wherever it is found. But this is not the gulf war in 1991. It is not the Iraq war in 2003, and that is true for a number of reasons.

Number one, U.S. ground troops will not be sent into combat in this conflict. From the last decade, we know that a sustainable strategy is not U.S. ground forces. It is enabling local forces to do what they have to do for themselves and for their country.

I want to be clear. The United States troops that have been deployed to Iraq, do not and will not, have a combat mission. Instead, they will support Iraq Forces on the ground as they fight for their country against these terrorists.

And in Syria, the on-the-ground combat will be done by the moderate opposition, which serves as the current best counterweight in Syria to extremists like ISIL. We know that ISIL, as it gets weaker, the moderate opposition will get stronger. And that will be critical in our efforts to bring about the political solution necessary to address the crisis in Syria once and for all.

That is one of the reasons why it is so critical that Congress authorize the opposition train-and-equip mission when it comes to the floor, but it is also critical that the opposition makes the most of the additional support, the kind of support that they have been requesting now for years. And they need to take this opportunity to prove to the world that they can become a viable alternative to the current regime.

Number two, this is more than just a military coalition, and I want to emphasize that. In some ways, some of the most important aspects of what we will be doing are not military. This mission is not just about taking out an enemy on the battlefield. It is about taking out a network, decimating and discrediting a militant cult masquerading as a religious movement. It is similar to what we have been doing to al-Qaeda these last years.

The bottom line is we will not be successful with a military campaign alone, and we know it. Nor are we asking every country to play a military role. We do not need every country to engage in that kind of military action, and frankly, we are not asking them and we do not want every country to do that. Only a holistic campaign will accomplish our objectives.

In addition to the military campaign, it will be equally important for the global coalition to dry up ISIL's illicit funding. And by the way, the Bahrainis, at the meeting in Jeddah, have offered to host a meeting—because they have been already engaged in this—that brings people together to focus on precisely the steps we can all take to do this, and that can positively have an impact not just on ISIL, but on other flows of terrorism support.

We have to stop the foreign fighters who carry passports from countries around the world, including the United States, and we also need, obviously, to continue to deliver urgently needed humanitarian assistance.

And finally, and this is really—you cannot overstate this. We must continue to repudiate the gross distortion of Islam that ISIL is spreading. Put an end to the sermons by extremists that brainwash young men to join these movements and commit mass atrocities in the name of God.

I was very encouraged to hear that Saudi Arabia's top clerics came out and declared terrorism a heinous crime under Sharia law and that the perpetrators should be made an example of. And I think—I might just mention—well, I will wait until we get in the Q and A. I will come back to this, but a very important statement was made today by the top clerics in the region, and I want to come back to that because I think it is critical.

But let me just emphasize that when we say global coalition, we mean it. And this is not—Australia, other countries, the Far East, countries in Europe have all taken on already initial responsibilities. So, my colleagues, we are committed to working with countries in every corner of the globe to match the campaign with the capabilities that we need to fight.

And I can tell you today that every single person I spoke to, in Wales at the Wales summit, in Jeddah, in Paris, where we had more than 30 countries and entities, they all expressed strong support for our mission and a willingness to help in some way. We had excellent meetings, and our meetings in Baghdad and in Cairo and in Ankara also advanced the process.

At the conference in Paris, we took another step toward the United Nations General Assembly (UNGA) meetings this week. And the UNGA meetings, unlike the meetings we have had thus far, which have all been behind closed doors, the UNGA meetings, these countries will be speaking out publicly at the United Nations Security Council, and the world will begin to see what each of these countries are prepared to do.

So we have a plan. We know the players. Our focus now is in determining what each country's role will be and how to coordinate those activities for success. Later this week, we are going to have more to say about our partners and the contributions, and we still fully expect this coalition to grow through UNGA and beyond.

One of the things that I am most pleased about is we have asked one of our most respected and experienced military leaders, General John Allen, to come to the State Department and oversee this effort. He came within 24 hours of being asked, was at his desk at 7 o'clock in the morning, and is now already laying out the campaign from a diplomatic point of view for how we coordinate what will be needed for all of these other aspects beyond the military piece.

And I had a long meeting with him yesterday, again today, and I am confident that together with Ambassador Brett McGurk, who will serve as his Deputy, and Assistant Secretary Anne Patterson, who was so much a part of our effort against al-Qaeda when she was our Ambassador to Pakistan, we have a very experienced group of people engaged in this effort. The fact is if we do this right, then this effort could actually become a model for what we can do with respect to the individual terrorist groups in other places that continue to wreak havoc on the efforts of governments to build their states and provide for their people.

And I am confident that with our strategy in place and our international partners by our side, we will have all that we need, and with the help of the Congress, we will be able to succeed in degrading and ultimately destroying this monstrous organization wherever it exists.

I know that was a little long, Mr. Chairman, but I wanted to lay it out, and I appreciate your patience.

[The prepared statement of Secretary Kerry follows:]

PREPARED STATEMENT OF SECRETARY OF STATE JOHN F. KERRY

Chairman Menendez, Ranking Member Corker, and members of the committee, thank you for holding this hearing on an issue where the stakes are so high and a full understanding of the ISIL threat and our strategy for defeating it is so important.

During the years I had the privilege of serving here, working with different administrations, it always struck me that American foreign policy works best when there's a genuine discussion, a dialogue, a vetting of ideas back and forth between Congress and the executive branch. So I want to make sure that by the time we're done here today, I've heard from you, you've shared your views and ideas, and that you also have a clear understanding of what we've done so far, what we're doing now, and where we go next—because your input and your support are absolutely critical to the success of this effort.

I want to underscore at the start—there are some debates of the past 20 years that could, and probably will, fill up books and documentaries for a long time. Iraq is one.

Iraq has caused some of the most heated debates and deepest divisions of the past decade—a series of difficult issues about which people can honestly disagree. But I didn't come here today to rehash those debates. The issue that confronts us today is one on which we should all agree: ISIL must be defeated. Period. End of story. And, collectively, we're all going to be measured by how we carry out this mission.

I'd also underscore—the same is true on an international level. And even in a region that is virtually defined by division, leaders who have viewed the last 11 years very differently—and who agree on very little in general—are more unified on this subject than just about any other.

So as President Obama described last week when he spoke directly to the American people, we have a clear strategy to degrade, defeat, and destroy ISIL. But the United States will not go it alone. That is why we are building a global coalition. And as I traveled around the world this week, the question foreign leaders were asking me was not whether they should join the coalition, but how they can help.

We are also not starting from scratch. This is an effort we have been building over time, both on our own and with the help of our international partners: Even before President Obama delivered his speech last week, nearly 40 countries had joined in contributing to the effort to strengthen the capacity of Iraq including military assistance, training, and humanitarian assistance.

We have been focused on ISIL since its inception as the successor to AQI in 2013. Back in January we ramped up our assistance to the Iraqi Security Forces, increasing our intelligence surveillance reconnaissance, or ISR, flights to get a better picture of the battlefield and expediting weapons like Hellfire missiles for the Iraqis to bring to bear in this fight.

Early this summer, the ISIL threat accelerated when it effectively erased the Iraq-Syria border and the Mosul Dam fell. The President acted deliberately and decisively. We further surged our ISR missions over Iraq. We immediately set up joint operation centers in Baghdad and Erbil. And our special forces conducted a very detailed field assessment of Iraqi Security Forces and Kurdish forces.

By the time ISIL launched the offensive in the north, President Obama authorized limited air strikes against ISIL and humanitarian missions to protect American personnel, prevent major catastrophes and support Iraqi Security Forces and Kurdish forces that were fighting bravely to do the same. To date, we've launched more than 150 airstrikes. And it is because of the platforms we put in place back in June that those strikes have been highly precise and incredibly effective, including in the operations to break the siege of Sinjar Mountain, retake Mosul Dam, and resupply the town of Amerli.

These actions blunted ISIL's momentum and created time and space for us to put in place the two pillars of a comprehensive strategy against ISIL: an inclusive Iraq Government, and a broad international coalition.

We redoubled our efforts to help move the Iraqi political process forward. We are clear-eyed about the fact that any strategy against ISIL would only succeed with a strong, inclusive government in Iraq, with an ambitious national agenda, prepared to unite the country against ISIL.

With our support, after several weeks of complex negotiations, President Masum nominated Haider al-Abadi to serve as Prime Minister. Shortly thereafter, Prime Minister al-Abadi—again with our support—was able to form his Cabinet and present it to the Parliament, and, last week, that government was approved.

This was a long and difficult process, led by the Iraqis, with our help as needed. The result was something Iraq had never before seen in its history: an election deemed credible by the United Nations, followed by peaceful transition of power, without any U.S. troops on the ground.

I traveled to Baghdad last week, immediately after the new government was approved, to meet with Prime Minister al-Abadi and other leaders throughout the Iraqi Government. And I was very encouraged to hear them discuss in detail the government's National Plan to unite the country against ISIL, and empower local communities—particularly in Sunni areas—to mobilize, defeat ISIL, and maintain security control in their area.

Throughout the entire process, we were in touch with regional leaders to ensure that a new and inclusive government would receive support from the region. Today, after years, even decades, of relative isolation from their neighbors, the Iraqis have begun to reintegrate with the broader Arab community. For example, last week, they were not just invited but warmly welcomed in Saudi Arabia, and the Saudis have now said they'll reopen an embassy in Baghdad.

With this new, inclusive Iraqi Government in place, it's time for the defensive strategy we and our international partners have pursued thus far to transition to an offensive strategy—one that harnesses the capabilities of the entire world to eliminate the ISIL threat, once and for all.

President Obama outlined this strategy in detail, so—while I am happy to answer any questions you may have—I will be brief in walking through it again now.

At its core, our strategy is centered on a global coalition that will collaborate closely across a number of specific areas—including, certainly, on direct and indirect military support.

To be clear, military assistance comes in a range of forms, from training and equipping, to logistics and airlift. And countries from inside and outside of the region are already providing support in these veins. So I have no doubt whatsoever we will have the capabilities and the resources we need to succeed militarily. And President Obama made clear we will be expanding the military campaign to take on ISIL in Iraq, in Syria—wherever it is found.

But this is not the gulf war in 1991, and it is not the Iraq war in 2003—for a couple of reasons. Number one, U.S. ground troops will not be sent into combat in this conflict. From the last decade we know that a sustainable strategy is not U.S.

ground forces—it is enabling local forces to do what they must for themselves and their country. I want to be clear: the U.S. troops that have been deployed to Iraq do not and will not have a combat mission. Instead, they will support Iraqi Forces on the ground as they fight for their own country against these terrorists.

And in Syria, the on-the-ground combat will be done by the moderate opposition—which serves as the best counterweight in Syria to extremists like ISIL. We know that as ISIL gets weaker, this moderate opposition will get stronger, which will be critical in our efforts to bring about the political solution necessary to address the crisis in Syria once and for all. That's one of the reasons why it's so critical that Congress authorizes the opposition train-and-equip mission when it comes to the floor. But it's also critical that the opposition makes the most of the additional support—the kind of support they've been requesting for years—and take this opportunity to prove to the world that they can be a viable alternative to Assad.

Number two, this is more than just a military coalition because the objective requires more than a military victory. This mission isn't just about taking out an enemy on the battlefield. It's about taking out an entire network—decimating and discrediting a militant cult masquerading as a religious movement.

It's similar to what we have been doing to al-Qaeda these last years.

The bottom line is we will not be successful with a military campaign alone. Nor are we asking every country to play a military role—we don't need every country to play a military role and we don't want every country to play a military role.

Only a holistic campaign can accomplish our objectives. That is why we are focused on multiple lines of effort.

In addition to the military campaign, it will be equally important for the global coalition to dry up ISIL's illicit funding, to stop the foreign fighters who carry passports from countries around the world including the United States, to continue to deliver urgently needed humanitarian assistance, and finally, to repudiate the gross distortion of Islam that ISIL is spreading, and put an end to the sermons by extremists that brainwash young men to join these movements and commit mass atrocities in the name of God. I was very encouraged to hear that Saudi Arabia's top clerics came out and declared terrorism a ''heinous crime'' under Sharia law—and that perpetrators should be made an example of. Preventing an individual from joining ISIL for example, or from getting to the battle field in the first place, is the most effective measure we can take.

I want to emphasize—when we say ''global coalition,'' we mean it. This is not a threat that a single country or region can take on alone. And there is a critical role for nearly every country to play.

So we are committed to working with countries in every corner of the globe to match the campaign's requirements with the capabilities they are willing to bring to bear.I spent the past week in the Middle East and in Europe, meeting with dozens of leaders whose partnership will be essential to our success.

And I can tell you today: every single person I spoke to over the course of my trip expressed strong support for our mission and a willingness to help in some way. We had excellent meetings, beginning at the NATO summit in Wales, and then in Jeddah. The Jeddah Communique represents a strong, comprehensive and unified statement of all the ways in which the region is committed to supporting this fight. Our meetings in Baghdad, in Cairo, and in Ankara also advanced the process. And at the conference earlier this week in Paris, we took another step along the road to the UNGA and the UNSC sessions next week.

We have a plan and we know the players. Our focus now is determining what role each country will play.

Later this week we will have more to say about our partners and contributions, and we fully expect the coalition to grow, evolve, and coalesce well beyond UNGA. That's why we've asked one of our most respected and experienced military leaders—Gen. John Allen—to come to the State Department and oversee this effort. And he's already hitting the ground running—he was at work last Friday at 7 am, less than 24 hours after we sealed the deal for him to do this job, and he and I had a long meeting yesterday, just a few hours after I landed in D.C. General Allen will be working with one of our foremost Iraq experts, Ambassador Brett McGurk, as well as Assistant Secretary Anne Patterson, who was so much a part of the effort against al-Qaeda when she was our Ambassador in Pakistan.

The fact is that, if we do this right, then this effort could become a global model for isolating and undermining other extremist threats around the world. But now we must be laser-focused on ISIL. And I'm confident that, with our strategy in place and our international partners by our side, we will have all that we need to succeed in degrading and ultimately destroying this monstrous organization—wherever it exists.

The CHAIRMAN. Well, thank you, Mr. Secretary.

Let me start off with I think one of the most critical lessons that we have learned from past U.S. military interventions abroad is that we must have a clear vision for the end state that we are seeking and a coherent strategy that is focused about how not only do we enter and succeed, but how do we exit a theater of war.

So I would like to get, as succinctly as you can, a statement from you as to what does the end goal look like. I heard you talk about taking out a network. I get that. But beyond that, what is the political end state conditions we are seeking so that we will know that it is time to end military action?

Secretary KERRY. Well, the military action ends when we have ended the capacity of ISIL to engage in broad-based terrorist activity that threatens the state of Iraq, threatens the United States, threatens the region. That is our goal. And that means ending their ability to live in ungoverned spaces, have a safe haven, and be able to control territory and move at will to try to attack the United States or other places.

The threat, obviously, right now is more immediate to the Middle East and to Europe, but we have Americans over there fighting with passports.

The CHAIRMAN. So, obviously, that does not mean we are going to look to eliminate every person who is associated with ISIL.

Secretary KERRY. We have not been able to eliminate every person associated with al-Qaeda.

The CHAIRMAN. Absolutely. So then the question——

Secretary KERRY. But we have been able to reduce their capacity to mount a major attack under the circumstances that we are able to obviously guard against, and engage in, preventive actions——

The CHAIRMAN. So, in Iraq, we want a sovereign Iraq whose territorial integrity has been restored without the presence of ISIL.

Secretary KERRY. And an independent, inclusive government that is functioning.

The CHAIRMAN. And in Syria?

Secretary KERRY. In Syria likewise. We believe that, ultimately, there is no solution to Syria without a political settlement. That goal has not changed. But Assad has had little incentive to negotiate.

The incentive that existed when I first went to Moscow last year, and President Putin and Russia agreed to support the Geneva process, regrettably got sidetracked by a number of things, one of which was the in-fighting that began to take place in the opposition itself. Two, the unexpected degree to which Assad became an extraordinary magnet for terrorists, and that is when you began to have this amazing flow of foreign fighters who came to get rid of Assad.

And as Assad gassed people and barrel bombed people and tortured and so forth, it became more evident to those global fighters, and particularly to countries in the region, they were focused on whatever group could get rid of Assad. And unfortunately, tragically, ISIL is somewhat an outgrowth of that phenomenon.

And therefore, we are today—you know, I think all the countries in the region have recognized that there was a mistake of judgment with respect to that process, and I think people are bending over backwards to try to rectify it.

The CHAIRMAN. I think members of this committee who joined together to first vote for the authorization of use of military force as President Obama was headed to the G20 summit at the time in Russia to deter Assad from using chemical weapons and who subsequently voted in a bipartisan effort to arm the vetted Syrian rebels over a year ago fully appreciate that.

It is my hope that when we refine the definition of the end state as it relates to the campaign against ISIL that we understand that if I am a moderate vetted rebel and I am being asked to fight against ISIL now, I also need to fight against Assad because that is my ultimate mission. And so, as we move forward, I would like to hear how that is coinciding.

Let me ask you two other questions. I heard you very clearly when you said we are not asking all of our partners to engage in direct military actions, but I hope that there will be, and I would like to hear from you, can we expect part of the Sunni Arab coalition members to, in fact, be part of military actions in this regard? Because this cannot be simply a campaign by the West against the East.

Secretary KERRY. You are absolutely correct, Mr. Chairman. And first of all, let me thank you and I thank the committee for the vote that you took, the only entity in the Congress that did. And it was an affirmative vote, and we are grateful for that and respect it.

Currently, there are countries outside of Europe and outside of the region committed to engage in military action. There are countries in Europe committed to take military action. There are countries in the region, Arab countries, committed to take military action.

We will have sufficient levels of commitment to take military action. It will be up to CENTCOM and General Allen and others to work on the question of who will do what.

The CHAIRMAN. It is fair to say that this is going to be a multiyear effort?

Secretary KERRY. Well, the President has been very clear about that. Certain parts of it will be, absolutely. I cannot tell you—I can tell you this. When we took them on at Mosul Dam and the Iraqis were on the ground and took them on, we took back Mosul Dam. When we took them on at Amirli, they moved out. When we took them on at Sinjar Mountain, we freed the people at Sinjar Mountain.

And we have currently enabled people to be able to hold them off at Haditha Dam, and it is clear from the intelligence we pick up that what we are doing now, which has fundamentally been more defensive than offensive, has already had an impact on them. I am convinced that with the proper effort, we can have an impact.

The CHAIRMAN. I do not dispute that you have had in the short term an impact to stem their advances, at least within the region that they are in. My question, though, is no one reasonably can come from the administration and suggest that the ultimate goal, which is taking out this network, is not going to be a multiyear effort?

Secretary KERRY. It is a multiyear effort. The President has already said that.

The CHAIRMAN. With that as a reality, then let me turn to the AUMF. How is it that the administration believes that—and I support its efforts. But how is it that the administration believes that the 9/11 AUMF or the Iraq AUMF provide the authorization to move forward whether the Congress decides to or not?

You know, it was not too long ago that members of the administration appeared before the committee, and when I asked them, I was headed toward repealing the Iraq AUMF. And there were administration witnesses who believed that it should be repealed on behalf of the administration. How is it that the administration now thinks it can rely upon that for legal authority?

Secretary KERRY. Mr. Chairman, how is it? It is because good lawyers within the White House, within the State Department, who have examined this extremely closely have come to the conclusion across the board that the 2001 AUMF, which says all necessary and appropriate force against those nations, organizations, or persons responsible for 9/11, those who harbored such organizations or persons, to prevent future acts of international terrorism against the United States by such persons or organizations, includes al-Qaeda. It has always been interpreted as including al-Qaeda. And al-Qaeda and——

The CHAIRMAN. Al-Qaeda threw out ISIL——

Secretary KERRY. But al-Qaeda and associated forces, that is the language. Al-Qaeda and associated forces. Now al-Qaeda, ISIL began as al-Qaeda. In 2005 in Iraq, 2004, ISIL was Al Qaeda in Iraq. And it only became this thing called ISIL a year ago, and it only became that out of convenience to separate themselves in an internal fight, but not because their thinking changed, not because their targets changed, not because their actions changed.

They are the same people doing—the same people that we were prepared to and were attacking for all of those years. And a mere publicity stunt to separate yourself and call yourself something else does not get you out from under the force of the United States law——

The CHAIRMAN. I appreciate your ability as a former prosecutor and a gifted attorney to try to make the case. I will tell you——

Secretary KERRY. Well——

The CHAIRMAN [continuing]. That at least from the chair's perspective you are going to need a new AUMF, and it will have to be more tailored because I do not want to be part of 13 years later and multitude of countries that have been used in this regard, for that to be the authority. And I think our goals are the same. I think we need to get you a different set of authorities, and I look forward to working with my colleagues——

Secretary KERRY. Not only are our goals the same, Mr. Chairman, but we know you are thinking about retooling the AUMF, and we welcome. We would like Congress, please, do this. We want that to happen. We are not going to make our actions dependent on it happening, but we will work with you as closely as we can and should in order to tailor an AUMF going forward, and we look forward to that opportunity.

The CHAIRMAN. Senator Corker.

Senator CORKER. Thank you, Mr. Chairman.

I just want to say, as I have said to you personally, we have three Senators—the President, Vice President, Secretary of State—that are exercising terrible judgment right now. And to say that you are going to do this regardless of what we say, you are not going to ask for buy-in by the United States Senate or House of Representatives on behalf of the American people in a conflict that you say is going to be multiyear, some people say a decade, taking us into another country with a different enemy is exercising the worst judgment possible.

And so, I have said this to you as strongly as I can personally. That is in essence what you are saying to the chairman right now. Saying "if Congress wants to play a constructive role we would welcome that" to me is a political game. And I am disappointed that you, as Secretary of State, after being chairman of this committee, after espousing the views that you have espoused in the past, out of convenience and parsing legal words would make the statement you just made.

So let me move on and say I would love—you say much has been accomplished. That is a nice photograph on the front of the Wall Street Journal. Tell me what has been accomplished. What Arab Sunni nation is going to have a ground force in Syria? What Arab Sunni country is going to be flying in and bombing and doing missile raids with an Arab insignia on the side of the plane? Tell me that.

Secretary KERRY. Senator, you will hear that at the appropriate time within the next days, as John Allen and the team work with all of these countries for the permissions, for the basing, for all the things that will take place. I have told you they have——

Senator CORKER. Let me ask you this.

Secretary KERRY. No, no, no. Let me——

Senator CORKER. Are you convinced that that will happen?

Secretary KERRY. Let me finish.

Senator CORKER. Are you convinced that that will happen?

Secretary KERRY. Well, I have already said that. I——

Senator CORKER. So we will have Arab Sunni countries participating in the ground effort in Syria?

Secretary KERRY. No, I did not say the ground effort, and you know, right now the plan is to work through the—and our judgment is that we can be effective working in the way that we are. Let me say a couple of things, first of all, with respect to your——

Senator CORKER. Well, you can say the answer to my questions, okay?

Secretary KERRY. Well, no, when I——

Senator CORKER. I am not going to be filibustered——

Secretary KERRY. No, I am going to answer your question. I am going to answer your question.

Senator CORKER. Okay.

Secretary KERRY. And I am sure the chair will be, you know, happy to have the kind of dialogue I talked about earlier. It is important to talk this through.

Senator CORKER. I have got 2 minutes and 34 seconds and 4 more questions.

Secretary KERRY. Well, Senator, you have not let me answer any of them yet. So let me try to answer the question.

Senator CORKER. Well, the question is what Arab Sunni country is going to be putting boots on the ground in Syria against this now-claimed army by your——

Secretary KERRY. At this moment, no country has been asked to put boots on the ground or no country is talking of it. And we do not think it is a good idea right now. So there is no discussion of that at this moment.

Now with respect to the judgment about asking Congress to do it, I am asking. Do it. Pass it. We would love to have you do it. But we are not going to get stuck in the situation, when we have the authority, of not exercising our authority to do what we believe we need to do to protect the country.

So we are asking you to do it. Pass it tomorrow.

Senator CORKER. You are asking us to do it, but you are not giving any details because you do not have them.

Secretary KERRY. That is not true, Senator.

Senator CORKER. Well, then share them.

Secretary KERRY. Senator, I am not going to share them in public here today. Many of these things——

Senator CORKER. Share them in a classified setting.

Secretary KERRY. I am confident there will be so many classified briefings that you will be tired of them. But at the moment, we are not going to lay this out until John Allen has had a chance to come to the U.N. on Friday, until we have had a chance to work closely with all of these countries in order to make this as effective as possible.

Senator CORKER. Do you realize how unserious the things that you have laid out and the things that were laid out yesterday sound when you are discussing training 5,000, in your all's own words, doctors and dentists and others in Saudi Arabia over a year? I do not know whether they are being trained for offensive or defensive—I would like you to clarify that—activities. My understanding is that they will be given higher tech equipment after they prove themselves on the battlefield.

Do you understand how unrealistic and how that effort on the ground where they are based, where ISIL is based, does not match the rhetoric that the administration has laid out? And therefore, you are asking us to approve something that we know the way you have laid it out makes no sense.

We have a strong sense that our Army, our military leaders have urged you to put special forces on the ground, but, no, we are not going to do that. So this does not even seem serious. It seems like a political answer to the United States as they cry out about this uncivilized activity, but it does not seem real to me.

And if you are willing to get in a classified setting and lay out all these details and tell us which of these countries are going to be flying their flag into Syria, they are going to be putting people on the ground. Because we know. We know the Free Syrian Army cannot take on ISIL. You know that.

You talk about a multiyear process. We are talking decades if that is going to be our salvation. So I will just close with this. I am disappointed. I was disappointed in the briefing we had last week.

I do want us to deal with this in an effective way. You have not laid it out in a way that meets that test. I hope when we come back and before you put people in harm's way unnecessarily, you have a plan that achieves the end that you just laid out. But we know right now that is not where you are.

And again, I hope you will seek it, I hope you will say that you are not going to do it without it, and I hope you will lay out a plan that will convince us that you are serious about doing the things you said you were going to do to the American people and to us about ISIL because you have not done it now. And I hope you will lay out a way to pay for it, to pay for it, because we know this is going to take many, many years, and it has to do with the safety of our citizens.

Secretary KERRY. Mr. Chairman, can I, I hope, answer a little bit here?

Senator, you know, I must say to you I really find it somewhat surprising for you to suggest that as the President of the United States talks to the Nation and commits to take strikes in order to deal with ISIL, as we have come back from a week of very serious meetings with nations around the world, all of whom are committed to this, that you sit there and suggest that it is not serious.

Now, with all due respect to you, Senator, let me just tell you something point blank. The moderate opposition in Syria has, in fact, been fighting ISIL for the last 2 years. And since last January, the Free Syrian Army has been engaged with ISIL in Idlib, in Aleppo, in the Damascus countryside, in Deir al-Zor, and groups such as the Syrian Revolutionary Front have fought off ISIL. They have expelled them from Idlib province, which borders Turkey and includes the border crossing.

Over the past 2 months, moderate brigades have been deployed in northern Aleppo to prevent ISIL from capturing key border towns, including Azaz, through which a large quantity of humanitarian assistance is now being sent. But they require our support.

Senator McCain knows that. He has been screaming about it for some time.

Senator CORKER. We have all been screaming about it, and you all have done nothing, or at least not much to talk about.

Secretary KERRY. Senator, let us just understand that the fact is that what has propelled ISIS to some degree is a word called success. And as ISIS has had success, they have used social media and they have appealed to greater numbers of greater fighters.

As they have now suddenly been put on their heels and as the United States and other countries do seriously commit to this endeavor—and believe me, what we are doing is serious—then if success begins to turn and move toward the Free Syrian Army and the moderate opposition, I believe you will see greater numbers of recruits. That is why the President is asking for that open training under Title X in order to try to build that up as fast as possible.

Our estimates are there are now currently tens of thousands still of fighting members of the opposition. And if you can get more people better trained, and by the way, every month that I have been Secretary of State, we have been adding to the effort of what we are doing with respect to the Syrian opposition, and most of that needs to be covered in a classified setting, as you know.

But our assessment is that we can and, given the urgency of the situation, begin to move this program to a greater degree. So will it take a period of time? We have all said that; yes. But we are confident that we have the ability to be able to change the situation on the ground.

The CHAIRMAN. Senator Boxer.

Secretary KERRY. By the way, I do have a list here. I am not going to go into all of it now. But there are Albania has sent in the last—we have had at least 18 flights that we have taken in to Erbil. We have been providing additional weapons to Peshmerga.

Other countries have been doing this. Australia has committed a number of different items to this. I am not going to go into them publicly. Bulgaria is providing aid. Canada, several—sending various kinds of assistance. Croatia, Czech Republic, Denmark, Estonia, France, Germany, Hungary, Italy, Saudi Arabia, Germany.

Look, there are a lot of countries here. And by the way, they are all serious, too, or they would not be on this list.

The CHAIRMAN. Senator Boxer.

Senator BOXER. Secretary Kerry, thank you for your tireless work.

I think it is shocking and a sad state of affairs that we heard just now such angry comments aimed at you, Mr. Secretary, and through you at our President, instead of at ISI, a savage terrorist group that decapitated two Americans and has warned—and I quote—that they will ''quench'' their thirst for American blood.

I think it is shocking. I am actually shaking and trembling. This is not the time to show anger at the people who are working night and day, whether you agree with them or not, to protect our people.

Now I want to talk about the AUMF. I voted against the one in 2002, which started the disastrous war in Iraq. I voted for the one in 2001, and I have reread it about six times.

Mr. Secretary, the lawyers I have consulted with believe that you have the authority to go after ISIL. It is very clear. You read the parts. If people listened to you, you read the parts that are correct.

Now that is not to say that I would not welcome working on a new AUMF. But I want to say right now, the way things get filibustered around this place and the way politics gets played around this place, I am proud that you say you are going to do your work to protect the American people.

This is just a sad opening of a hearing. I have never seen it, and I have gone through some tough ones.

Now I want to say this. The Iraq war inflamed the long-simmering sectarian divisions in that country. I know you do not want to get into the past. It is fine. I think it is worth mentioning because from my point of view, that is a war I voted against. I am for going after ISIL because there is such a difference.

And there are two strains of thought as people speak out against the policy of the administration. One is they say you are not doing enough. Go back with those ground troops, more war, more boots on the ground. American boots, they are the only boots that work. You have proven just with a few examples that it is just not true, and I certainly reject that view.

And the other, the second school of thought represented by some of the folks out there who I like and talk to all the time, they think we should not take the fight to ISIL. Forget it. It is too complicated. It is fraught with uncertainty. We should sit on the sidelines. I oppose that view as well.

You cannot sit on the sidelines, at least I cannot, when you have a group that is selling 14-year-olds, as my former colleague said. Selling 14-year-old girls as slaves, giving them as gifts to their fighters, murdering ethnic and religious minorities, including Christians, Yazidis, and Shiite Turkmen. And again, warning that their ''knife will continue to strike the necks'' of Americans.

They have a very simple goal. They say if you do not take our twisted version of Islam, you either flee, you convert, or you die. So, no, I am not going to sit idly by.

Mr. Secretary, I have a question for you. I was being interviewed, and I was expressing these views that I was just expressed that there were certain areas where it is gray, and there are certain areas where it is clear to me. I mean, everyone takes their own lens to the question.

And I was asked this question. How can we make sure that the Syrian moderates we help are the right ones? And this particular reporter said, well, we have heard reports that the Syrian moderates signed a nonaggression pact with ISIL.

My answer to that was there are all kinds of Syrian moderate groups, and we are certainly not working with those who do not see it our way. Could you expand on that answer or——

Secretary KERRY. I would be delighted to. Let me just say to you that is disinformation fundamentally put out by ISIL. The moderate opposition recently restated its commitment as a national movement to fighting extremism generally and including ISIL. And a recent statement that they had reached a truce is simply baseless, not accurate, and they have not. And they will not.

Senator BOXER. Thank you.

And then just, I mean, I do not have enough time to ask everything. So I will ask one last question. What roles do Iran and Russia play in this conflict, and how do the interests of these two countries factor into the President's counter-ISIL strategy? I know it is very delicate, but how would you respond to that?

Secretary KERRY. Well, you know, Russia, obviously, is a principal line of support to Assad, and Assad, as we all know, has neither proven the willingness nor the capacity to go after ISIL. And Russia was at the meeting in Paris. China was at the meeting in Paris. Both spoke out powerfully about the need to stand up to ISIL.

And Iran, as you know, there was the subject of whether or not they might have been invited. There were certain problems in trying to make that happen because of country objections with respect to their presence, et cetera, and it did not happen. But Iran, obviously, is deeply opposed to ISIL.

Now we are not coordinating militarily or doing anything, but we have had brief conversations on the side of our negotiations that are taking place, the P5+1 Iran nuclear negotiations. And we are prepared to see whether or not Iran can contribute in a constructive way. But that would require also changing what is happening in Syria, where their IRGC is on the ground and supporting Assad and been engaged in activities, Hezbollah on their behalf, whom they support.

So there are a lot of areas of twisted conflict in the relationships here, and we are looking—you know, it would be negligent not to be open to listening to some change in the dynamic or some possibility of constructive activity. But we are not relying on it, waiting for it, organizing around it, or in fact coordinating with it at this point in time.

Senator BOXER. Thank you.

The CHAIRMAN. Before I turn to Mr. Risch, Senator Risch, let me just say to the Secretary on this subject I heard what you said. But to me, Iran is a regional instigator. It is a patron of the murderous Assad regime. It is a sponsor of sectarian divisions inside of Iraq.

It uses Iraq's airspace to send troops and men into Syria, and some of us are really concerned that, first of all, their end purposes are not our end purposes. And secondly, that some of us are concerned that negotiations with Iran, you know, are affected by to the extent that they express any desire to be helpful, they want to do it at the cost of concessions at the negotiating table.

I know you are shaking your head, and I would not expect anything else.

Secretary KERRY. Not going to happen.

The CHAIRMAN. But I have to be honest with you, when we hear all these back channel efforts and then they get outed by the Ayatollah, it creates uncertainty in that process. So I do not want to take more time from my colleague, but Senator Risch?

Senator RISCH. Thank you, Mr. Chairman.

John, I share some of the anger of Senator Boxer when it comes to what has been going on with the beheading of Americans. I mean, this is a tough time for America—for Americans to be watching their fellow citizens being beheaded by these savage people, and something has got to be done about it.

And I fully empathize with the problem you have got to where it is happening is such a complex situation with complex cultures and what have you, and you have got to do something about it. I want to throw in with the chairman. He mentioned three points, I think, in his opening that he was hoping he would hear, and I have not heard yet.

And that is he talked about hearing the plan that you have, and he wanted to hear what success looks like, and he wanted to hear some metrics as to how we measure progress. And John, I am just not there yet. I am not convinced.

And this is particularly true where I think everyone is in agreement. The President is in agreement. Congress is in agreement. The American people are in agreement. Nobody wants boots, American boots on the ground. I mean, that just is not going to happen. There is nobody—nobody going to go there with that.

In fact, had the President come here and said that, look, I want authorization for airstrikes. You and I both know how effective the drone program has been and how good it has been as far as accomplishing the goals that we have in Yemen, in Pakistan, and in other places. If he would have come here for that, you would have had no problem with me.

As far as the boots on the ground, who do you get to do it? Well, we know the Iraqis cannot do it. They dropped their guns and uniforms and went home at the slightest bit of threat. With all due respect, I know everybody talks about the moderates, opposition and the rebels. We have been through this for over a year, and I am just not convinced that there is such a group there.

So you said let us talk about this, and let us see if we cannot come up with some way to do this. You know, the best group around to be able to do this for boots on the ground are the Kurds. They have been incredibly successful. They have been a reliable— they have been reliable to us. They are great fighters.

I mean, if anybody is going to succeed on the ground in Iraq or, for that matter, in Syria, it is going to be the Kurds. Have you guys given thought to partnering up with them? What am I missing here?

Secretary KERRY. Well, you are not, Senator. They have been extraordinary, and that was our first line of effort, obviously. That is why we put the joint operation center in Erbil right away. And that is why we elicited immediate support. We really had to hold that line.

That was critical, and that is why the President was prepared to use some strikes, actually, to help guarantee that that happened. And there is a huge flow of weaponry. As I said, 18 flights that I know of from us have gone in now to Erbil. There are flights coming from other countries, too. Italians, others, lots of countries have been supporting the Kurds in this effort.

And you know, I think this is the work that John Allen needs a chance to sort of develop a little bit, see how it is going to go. The bottom line is the commitment to destroy ISIL, and that means what I described earlier today. And for the moment, growing the moderate opposition is one way of coming at it, and we will see, you know, what else may be possible as we go forward.

Senator RISCH. I appreciate that, and it is encouraging for me to hear that you have engaged the Kurds. I think that——

Secretary KERRY. Oh, very, very much so.

Senator RISCH. Let me with the little time I have left, I just want to make absolutely certain of your testimony. You originally said when you were meeting with these other countries, they have said, and I am quoting you, ''What can we do to help?'' But you have also said that nobody has agreed to put boots on the ground. And then I think you said that you have not asked them to put boots on the ground.

So let me be very clear about airstrikes. Has anybody committed that they would fly their flag in and do airstrikes into Syria?

Secretary KERRY. Yes.

Senator RISCH. And they are committed to do that?

Secretary KERRY. Yes.

Senator RISCH. Okay. That is good. In a classified setting, we will be able to get who those people are?

Secretary KERRY. Yes.

Senator RISCH. That is much more encouraging. Thank you. And with that, my time is up.

Thank you, Mr. Chairman.

The CHAIRMAN. Senator Cardin.

Senator CARDIN. Well, Secretary Kerry, first of all, thank you for your incredible service.

And what you have stated expresses my view on the need for international action against a barbaric terrorist organization, ISIL. It requires an international response. I think President Obama has been effective, particularly in the actions in Iraq. The military strikes have been very effective in pulling back ISIL's advancements, and I think the President deserves credit for doing that and certainly has my support.

You have been effective in bringing about an international coalition, and that is extremely important. Whenever we are involved in missions like this, it must include an international presence. And you have been very clear that we will not have combat ground troops as part of this campaign. And I support each of those statements.

So I want to get back to the point that the chairman mentioned, and I guess just about every one of us have mentioned, in regard to the authorization of force because I am not clear what we will do in Syria, and I am not comfortable yet as to what we will do in Syria. And I am looking forward to more information being made available to us.

But my concern, I would really like to get your thoughts on this, is that the authorizations that were passed in 2001 and 2002 were clearly aimed at a different circumstance. And if your lawyers' interpretations are correct, they are open-ended indefinitely, well beyond the Obama administration and could be used for long-term commitments, including ground force commitments in the future.

And that certainly was not congressional intent. I did not support the 2002 resolution. As the chairman said, it was based upon misinformation. And 2001 was clearly aimed at the circumstances in Afghanistan. It was not intended to deal with the current circumstances in Syria. I would hope we would all agree to that.

So I think it is absolutely essential that we come together and revisit the authorization issues. More than that you would welcome congressional involvement, I think it is imperative that we attempt to clarify the authorizations on the use of force to meet the current needs.

In Iraq, I do not think that is going to be difficult. I think you have been invited in by another country. I think we can——

Senator BOXER. You mean Iraq.

Senator CARDIN. I mean Iraq. Excuse me, in Iraq. I do not think it is difficult in Iraq. Thank you, Senator Boxer.

We have been invited in by the host country. It is clear we are not going to put combat troops on the ground there.

Syria is going to be more difficult because there are many of us who are not prepared to authorize the use of force in Syria with the information we currently have. But that is something I think we have to work with.

You have Article II power, and the President has Article II power. So he always has the right for a short period of time to defend the interests of this Nation as he sees fit, and that is his responsibility as Commander in Chief.

So I do not think there is any immediate urgency for congressional action. But I just think it is vital for the appropriate role of

Congress and for moving forward beyond just the Obama administration because, as you pointed out, these circumstances are not going to end in the next 2 years. And I would just welcome your thoughts as to how you think we should proceed with an authorization that can pass Congress and give you the comfort level that you need to protect us against any lengthy combat involvements in these countries in the future should ultimately be done by their own military?

Secretary KERRY. Sure. Well, Senator, thank you very much. Thank you for your comments.

But, look, I would not sit here comfortably and suggest to you— nor would President Obama, by that token, I know—suggest to you that this ought to go on indefinitely and that there should not be an effort with Congress to define this. Of course, there should be.

I think the American people want it, deserve it, and it is appropriate role for both branches to play, to work together to articulate that going forward. The President has made it crystal clear he is ready to do that. We know the chairman has announced that he is going to begin work to define that. We look forward to working with you to define it. That is how we go about it is to work effectively to do it.

Now in the immediate moment, we have a Prime Minister—do you have the comments of Prime Minister Abadi from the press conference the other day? Get those out for me, please.

[Pause.]

Secretary KERRY. In my meeting with Prime Minister Abadi, at the end we met with the press, and I will just read you what Prime Minister Abadi said as an opening comment, not even prompted or part of a question. He said, ''ISIL is a terrorist nation. It is mobilizing its international network to recruit people from all over the world. They have funds from all across the region. We are fighting these people. These people are—'' and then something inaudible about our communities attacking or something, minorities, women, children. ''They already—'' and then it was inaudible about women and killing or raping. ''They are a challenge to the whole region, to the international community. They are coming to Iraq from across the border from neighboring Syria. Of course, our role is to defend our country, but the international community is responsible to protect Iraq and protect Iraqis and the whole region.

''What is happening in Syria is coming across to Iraq. We cannot cross that border.'' That is on an international basis. But he says, ''It is an international border, but there is a role for the international community, for the United Nations, to do that role and the United States to act immediately to stop the spread of this cancer. ''This cancer is spreading in the whole region, and we have the resolution to fight the cancer in Iraq. We Iraqis will have both an inclusive government now, and we can do this job properly, everybody as whole.''

And he goes on to talk about how they will do it. But he specifically asks for the United States of America to help in this role.

Now our lawyers also are clear that Iraq has the right of self-defense, and Iraq is exercising its right of self-defense and asking the United States to help it. And we already have a military agreement with them with respect to that. And so, Iraq is asking us to help them.

And as a matter of right, if they are being attacked from outside their country, you have a right of hot pursuit. You have a right to be able to attack those people who are attacking you as a matter of self-defense.

So we believe there is a full justification here, and obviously, that will be laid out further. But is it better to have a greater statement of that? Is it better to have the Congress of the United States defining this going forward? We agree. But we need to move and to move rapidly because of the urgency of this danger.

The CHAIRMAN. Senator Rubio.

Senator RUBIO. Thank you.

Secretary Kerry, I was struck by the language in your opening statement. ''ISIL must be defeated, period. End of story. And collectively, we are all going to be measured by how we carry out this mission.''

Now from a military perspective, the plan of carrying out this mission involves a combination of Iraqi Forces in Iraq, from the military perspective more capacity; of course, the Kurds; moderate rebels in Syria; and American airpower. No combat boots on the ground on the part of the United States.

But over the last few days since the President has made that announcement, there has been real doubts expressed by military experts over whether that strategy will achieve what you have defined as our goal. The Washington Post reported that the top U.S. commander in the Middle East advised the President that we needed a modest contingent of American troops, especially Special Operation Forces, to advise and assist Iraqi army units.

The Chairman of the Joint Chiefs yesterday in the Armed Services Committee said that if local forces do not work, he would recommend U.S. ground troops potentially to the President. So my question is if it becomes clear that the only way to achieve the defeat of ISIL, period, end of story, is for the engagement of American ground troops, will that be something the President will consider at that time?

Secretary KERRY. The President will not put American ground troops into Iraq, and the President made it clear again today in a statement that he made at CENTCOM that America can make a decisive—I am quoting the President. ''We can make a decisive difference, but I want to be clear. The troops that have been deployed to Iraq do not, and will not, have a combat mission.''

Now we believe—and we are not going to deal with hypotheticals about what happens if and this and this. We believe there are any number of options as to how one can guarantee the effect on ISIL long before you were to get to the hypothetical conversation about Americans.

So I understand the Chairman of the Joint Chiefs of Staff, whose job it is to look at it from his perspective in terms of his military and his judgment. But the President has made a judgment as Commander in Chief that that is not in the cards, and that is where we are.

Senator RUBIO. So even if the only way, with the military expert——

Secretary KERRY. I am not going to deal with a hypothetical. I do not believe it is the only way.

Senator RUBIO. Well, it is not a hypothetical. It is actually—it appears to be, quite frankly, we are relying on a military strategy built on rebels who, at this point, are under assault not just by ISIS, but by the Assad regime, by local Iraqi Forces, of which some testimony say up to half, are incapable of fighting at this stage, and Kurds that have been great fighters but are only willing to protect their territory.

This is a very clearly stated goal, and the reason why it is not a hypothetical is there may come a point where what you are saying is that if the only thing that can solve this problem is U.S. combat forces, we are not going to do that, and ISIL gets to stay.

Secretary KERRY. But I think we are so far away from that quote being the only way in a hypothetical. I mean, honestly.

Senator RUBIO. Then let me ask you this.

Secretary KERRY. No, let me just—let me just finish that. I mean, you know, I am not going to get into hypotheticals, but you are presuming that Iran and Syria do not have any capacity to take on ISIL. I mean, who knows? I am not going to get—I do not know what is going to happen here. Let us start down this road and see what happens.

Senator RUBIO. Well, let me ask you about that then. So what you are saying now is that there is the opportunity, the potential that the United States would be coordinating with Iran?

Secretary KERRY. No, I never said anything about coordinating. If we are failing and failing miserably, who knows what choice they might make. You prepositioned this on the notion we are failing. I do not believe we are going to fail.

Senator RUBIO. I did not preposition on——

Secretary KERRY. And we are not setting out——

Senator RUBIO. I am prepositioning on the state of the military——

Secretary KERRY. You did. You said if we fail we cannot do that.

Senator RUBIO. Well, again, I will go back to the report. I mean, a number of people, including former Defense Secretary Gates has expressed his belief that it is not possible. A number of highly qualified military experts have said they do not believe that the goal you have stated in your opening statement is achievable without a U.S. presence.

Secretary KERRY. There are lots of possibilities. There are lots of possibilities between here and there. The President has said he is not going to put American troops——

Senator RUBIO. Well, you mentioned Iran. And you know, Iran yesterday said that not that it was on the sidelines of these negotiations. They claim that the U.S. Ambassador in Iraq reached out to the Iranian Ambassador in Iraq and asked to discuss some sort of level of coordination.

And the Iranians already gave us our answer. You said you were open to some sort of dialogue with them if it had any sort of promise to be productive. He has already answered the question. He says he sees no point in coordinating with a country whose hands are dirty. That is what he said about us.

He says, quite frankly, that—he said this, not me, please. He said that you are lying, that we did not exclude them from the talks to join the coalition. They excluded themselves, that they refused to participate. And he went on to say that in Iraq, the United States goal is to turn it into a playground where we can enter freely and bomb at will.

I would just say that any hopes of coordinating with Iran, who I consider to be just as evil as ISIS, is something that I would discourage for a number of different reasons. But I want to ask you just one more question, and it has to do with the rebels in Syria.

Later today, Ambassador Ford is going to testify that the biggest enemy that moderate opposition faces is the Assad regime. In fact, there are credible reports today that the Assad regime has stepped up its targeting of moderate rebel or non-ISIS rebel forces in the hopes of wiping them out so that they, the Assad regime, will be the only alternative left in Syria.

If we are interested in supporting the moderate rebels, will it not require us to protect them from Syria as well, from the Assad regime as well, if we hope that they can develop into a credible fighting force?

Secretary KERRY. ISIL first. That is our policy.

Senator RUBIO. Well, but Ambassador Ford is going to testify later today that the biggest enemy they face is the Assad regime bombing them, and there are reports today, credible reports, that Assad has stepped up his campaign attacking these moderate rebels. They may not be there for us to arm.

Secretary KERRY. That is not our judgment, but we obviously recognize that there are serious challenges with the Assad regime, and our policy has not changed of opposing the Assad regime and helping the moderate opposition. And in classified forum, I think we have a better opportunity to discuss what we are doing additionally in order to do that.

The CHAIRMAN. Senator Shaheen.

Senator SHAHEEN. Thank you, Mr. Secretary, for being here and for all of your tireless efforts to address the ISIS threat.

That is a threat that I believe was really brought home to the American people by the barbarous and heinous murders of James Foley and Steven Sotloff. And as you may know, Jim Foley grew up in New Hampshire, and Steven Sotloff went to prep school there. And so, they both have ties to my State, and I think people in New Hampshire and across the country really felt very personally those murders.

I appreciate and I said this yesterday at the Armed Services hearing with General Dempsey and Secretary Hagel that I appreciate the efforts of our men and women in the military to make a rescue attempt to free those—James Foley and Steven Sotloff and the other Americans—being held hostage. But I have been very troubled by the comments from the Foley family that have been reported about their concern that they were not communicated with and did not have support from our government as they were trying to deal with the hostage situation for their son.

And I wonder if you could—well, let me rephrase this. I hope that post the murders that this administration and future administrations will seriously reassess what can better be done to support families who are dealing with this kind of a crisis. Some of the reports have pointed out that there are other countries who have different ways of dealing with the families, and I certainly hope that you will help in this effort as we look at how we can better support those families.

Secretary KERRY. Well, Senator Shaheen—excuse me. Senator Shaheen, first of all, let me begin by saying that I know how personally deeply involved you were in Jim's case and in working with us to try to keep the focus on it. I know how close you were to the family, and I know how much effort when into the prior effort when Jim was in Libya. I worked on that personally and on this subsequent effort.

We raised it with country after country to try to get a Foreign Minister or some contact in the country. Is there a way to get proof of life? Is there a way to find out where he is? Is there a way to negotiate the release?

Most recently, even in the last 2 months before he was barbarously killed, I was talking with people in one of the Middle Eastern countries who traveled to Syria on our behalf in order to try to find out whether there was a way to secure the release of these hostages. And we—I know that you also made an incredible effort to reach out to country after country. I know the Czech Republic, others, you were very much active in this and engaged in that.

And when we got him out of Libya, which we worked hard to do, I was in touch with people on global posts who I know very closely. I mean, they are friends of mine who are part of that effort. So they were always in touch with me and talking personally about it.

Now I have read these accounts of things that have happened or their judgment. I talked to Diane and John Foley after Jim was killed. I think everybody here would just shudder at what they have to go through.

So this is something we feel very deeply, so much so that I remember the hours we sat in the situation room in the White House working with our brilliant military, who did a remarkable job of designing a rescue mission, and the President made the difficult decision. Because it is always difficult. You are putting American service people at risk going into another country. They have air defense. You do not know what is going to happen. And you know you are going in where there is ISIL.

And I sat in the White House in the situation room and watched that entire mission unfold and was amazed by the capacity of our military people to do what they did. A high-risk mission performed flawlessly. And the intelligence was correct to every degree that they went the right place. They did things correctly. It just was empty.

They had moved them ahead of time, and we do not know exactly how soon or when. And you have no idea how just the feeling in that room changed when the message came from our people on the ground saying nobody is there. So we felt that and feel it to this day.

But you know, if they feel unhappy somehow that it was not worked properly, whatever agency it was, we have to make sure in the future that we are going to make sure that that is just not a feeling—I mean, first of all, we hope no other family has to suffer that and go through it.

But to whatever degree that is a possibility or an eventuality, we have got to make sure that people feel better about the process. And I can assure you the President on down, everybody feels that sensitivity.

Senator SHAHEEN. Well, thank you. I appreciate that. And for the hostages who are still being held, I hope there will be an effort to look at how those families are being supported.

Mr. Chairman, I know that my time is up. But I just wanted to make one more comment because I know, Mr. Secretary, that you have repeated the President's argument that this military campaign does not require a separate authorization for the use of military force. But I certainly believe that if we are going to commit to a long-term effort to address ISIS that having specific congressional action that is bipartisan to support that effort is very important.

And I believe we should undertake that, and I know the chairman has said that he intends to do that, regardless of whether the White House and the administration comes to Congress or not. So I certainly support that, and I hope that the administration will work with us as we do that.

Secretary KERRY. Yes. Well, we are coming to Congress. We are here, and we welcome it, and we look forward to working with you on it.

The CHAIRMAN. Thank you. And Senator Shaheen has expressed to me on more than one occasion already her desire to work with the chair and others on behalf of such an AUMF, and we look forward to working you and other colleagues as well.

Senator Johnson.

Senator JOHNSON. Thank you, Mr. Chairman. Mr. Secretary, obviously these are pretty complex issues. I do not envy you and the President your task at all. You are in my prayers. The President is in my prayers. Actually, I ask all Americans to include you in their prayers because if you succeed—we all want you to succeed—that means America and Americans remain safe.

I have been listening to you and the President very carefully. I am sure the world has been as well, and words have real meaning. So I appreciate the fact that you have testified today here that ISIL must be defeated period, end of story.

You know, the President in his speech to the Nation said that the goal here is to degrade and ultimately destroy ISIS, but here is my concern. Here is my problem. In the final—in the final two paragraphs of his speech to the Nation, President Obama said, ''Our own safety, our own security depends on our willingness to do what it takes to defend this Nation.'' But, Mr. Secretary, by taking options off the table, is President Obama not really saying to do what it takes up to a point?

And as Secretary of State, as you are dealing with potential coalition partners who are also listening, if we state a goal and the world does not believe we are 100 percent committed to it, is that going to be very difficult for you to get the kind of commitment out of our potential partners to do what they need to do to actually achieve that ultimate goal?

Secretary KERRY. That is a very fair and a really good question. And by the way, thank you for your comments and your prayers. The answer is that the President and the military folks currently believe we have the capacity, we have the plan, and we have the coalition to be able to do the job. Now, you know, there are a lot of countries in the region who have capacity going forward who, in our judgment, if somebody is necessary to be on the ground, ought to be lining up first. So there are a lot of options here before we start getting to the talk that the President has taken off the table.

Senator JOHNSON. So, okay. We have covered—we have covered that ground. Let me ask you. In our discussions with, for example, Saudi Arabia, do the potential Arab States, do they understand how fragile American public opinion will be toward this effort, toward this destruction, if they do not fully commit?

And when I think of fully commit, I am thinking back to the first gulf war when America only had to pay for about 15 percent of that, and almost 50 percent of that war effort was paid for by Gulf States. The other portion was paid for Germany and Japan. I mean, do they understand why it is so important for them to step up to the plate and visibly support this effort?

Secretary KERRY. Yes, and, in fact, King Abdullah said to me, personally, ''We will do whatever is needed to be done. We are committed fully to this effort,'' and they have been. Now, there are bigger complications than just sitting here and talking about having the Kingdom of Saudi Arabia put its troops on the ground in Syria next door to Iran with all of the extraordinary complications of the region regarding Shia, Sunni, and other geostrategic challenges.

So we need to be working at this very carefully with all of the nations that are part of the coalition, recognizing we have to win. And we are just getting started at that. So I can tell you we are not going into this in order to fail, and nor are any of these other people who are signing up, so.

Senator JOHNSON. Well, let me offer, I will be in—up in New York next week representing the United States at the U.N. with Senator Cardin. I would like to offer, you know, whatever I can do to help convince those Arab States that they do need to be fully committed to this battle.

Let me ask you another question. An analogy I have been using, and here is another concern of mine. If this is going to literally take years, the analogy I have been using is if you identify a hornet's nest in your backyard, you realize you have got to take care of that. But if what we are really doing is just going in the backyard and poking that hornet's nest with a stick, is that not a concern right now if we are not fully committed to wipe out ISIS quickly?

You mentioned Brett McGurk, who provided powerful testimony to this committee back at the end of July about the threat that ISIS really does represent, being able to funnel 30 to 50 suicide bombers into Iraq per month. Now, we have seen those suicide bombers come from Australia and Germany and America with passports. And Mr. McGurk's comment was they could easily funnel those suicide bombers into the West, into America.

So that is my concern about allowing this—not being fully committed, not getting in there, not cleaning up that hornet's nest as quickly as possible. Do we not just increase the time where we are really under threat and danger?

Secretary KERRY. Well, we hope not, Senator. Obviously that is not our strategy. I mean, look, ISIL—why do we have to focus first on ISIL and focus on it in the way that we are? Because they are seizing and holding thousands of square miles of territory; because they are claiming to be a state—they are not a state in so many ways, and we can go through that. They are confronting and defeating thus far a conventional army with conventional tactics. They have—they are avowed genocidists—avowed genocidists—who have already practiced genocidal activities at a certain level—Yazidis, Shia, people that they have decided to go after along the way—Christians. And they have a very large amount of money, unlike lots of other terrorist organizations because they cleaned out the banks, and they have sold oil, and done other things in the process.

And so, even al-Qaeda, bold as they were in what they decided to do, did not exhibit these characteristics and did not have those capacities. And that is why we believe—and we think most of the region has come to understand this, including the moderate opposition, who are already fighting ISIL.

So we believe we have the makings of an ability to be able to have a very, very significant impact. And already, by the way, France and the United Kingdom are flying with us over Iraq, and several other countries are now starting to be willing to join that. So we think we have the building of an ability to be able to turn that around.

I guarantee you the President's goal is to defeat them. And as you and we see this unfold and make judgments about how well we are doing, we can have further discussions about what else it may or may not take to get the job done. But at the moment, these are the judgments that are being made.

Senator JOHNSON. Well, thank you. You have made a strong case for defeating ISIS and being fully committed to doing it. The sooner the better. Thank you.

The CHAIRMAN. Senator Durbin.

Senator DURBIN. Thank you, Mr. Chairman. Thank you, Mr. Secretary. Mr. Secretary, as I look at this challenge from ISIL, I think there are two distinctly different parts to it relating to Iraq and Syria. I do not believe there is any future for Iraq unless Iraq is committed to that future.

The new leadership there has given us some hope, but ultimately we have to trust that we can either train or provide the skills and support to the Iraq Army that, in fact, they will not be so overrun with corruption that they cannot be an effective fighting force. That is—it is a big task, but I think it is—at least we are hopeful it is within our grasp.

I look at Syria and see a totally different circumstance there. Syria is a dog's breakfast of violence, and terrorism, and deceit, and carnage that has gone on for three years. Here we are talking about arming or equipping and training a moderate force within Syria. I have read the language that is being considered in the

House, unless it has been changed in the last day or so. Never mentions the word "Assad" once when it talks about what we are trying to achieve in Syria.

It comes down to this basic question. It looks to me that there are at least three identifiable forces in Syria: Assad, ISIL, and what we hope are moderate opposition forces we can work with. But I am also told and have been told there are up 1,500 different militia in that country. Some are neighborhood militia.

How can we chart a course here that defeats ISIL in Syria and does not in the end strengthen Assad's hand? How can we find the so-called moderate opposition in Syria and believe that something will merge there that results in Syrians deciding that their own fate and future is their responsibility?

Secretary KERRY. A very good question. The calculation is that even with the difficulties that they have faced over the last year and a half particularly—I remember when I first came in, February of last year, the opposition in Syria was actually in a slightly better position with respect to Assad and the other groups. And there were not as many of the other groups at that moment in time.

And then regrettably, they started to squabble politically as well as to which military group would do what, and they lost some momentum with that, number one. Number two, they did not get enough supplies at that point in time. Number three, the country began to be flooded with these external fighters from the outside, and some countries in the region who wanted to get rid of Assad started funding people who seemed to be tougher fighters who morphed into either al-Nusra, Ahrar ash-Sham, or ISIL, and then they began to fight. And so the concentration on Assad just dissipated, and during that time some of the support that was coming from countries in the region was frankly also very badly directed and managed.

All of that has changed now. We have upped our support and our engagement, our training, things that we are doing. Other countries have upped it. They have worked out many of the leadership issues that existed. There seems to be—even despite these difficulties, they have been able to fight ISIL, and move ISIL out of certain areas, and keep fighting Assad. You have seen this continuing.

Our belief, therefore, is that as the principal antagonist to their presence—more so than Assad in some ways—starts to take hits and they gain greater strength, greater training, greater equipment, greater capacity, the success will bring to them, we think, a larger structure as well as a greater know-how and ability. And if ISIL is defeated, they are going to be taking that experience in the same direction that they originally set out to, which is to deal with Assad.

Senator DURBIN. I would like to ask one last question. We know, and you have said it in this testimony, that Russia is supplying Assad. We have known in the past when there have been sources of money, equipment, and other support for our enemies.

As we look at ISIL today, you told us in testimony that Russia—you mentioned Russia—and China, and we know by its nature Iran is a Shia nation—oppose ISIL. Who are the countries—which countries are aiding and abetting the ISIL cause either by providing resources, equipment, and arms to them, or allowing their trade to create resources and wealth so that they can continue the fight?

Secretary KERRY. We do not believe at this point that it is state supported. What we believe is that because of their success in particularly getting the bank in Mosul and other success along the way, as well as in selling oil——

Senator DURBIN. Let me stop you there. Who are they selling it to? Which countries are transiting——

Secretary KERRY. I was just about to get to you. We have raised with a number of countries in the region the question of how they could possibly be getting oil out of the country. It is being smuggled out. And that is part of the approach here is to deal——

Senator DURBIN. Through which countries do you believe it is being smuggled out?

Secretary KERRY. Well, it is being smuggled out from the border countries of Syria obviously, which means either through Turkey or through Lebanon or south. That is how——

Senator DURBIN. Now, are they joining us in the effort to stop the smuggling?

Secretary KERRY. They are, but obviously Turkey has difficulties right now, has 49 hostages that are being held, and they have talked about that publicly. And Turkey is—you know, we have had some conversations with them, and those conversations will continue.

Senator DURBIN. The sooner we can cut them off from their sources of funds and——

Secretary KERRY. That is exactly what the objective—now, a lot of the money——

Senator DURBIN [continuing]. Arms.

Secretary KERRY. There is other money that comes through social media, Internet appeals, through individual fundraising. We have been able to trace a one-time lump sum, $140,000, that came through one country from an individual in the region. And that is why we are going to have this immediate focus on the movement of money, and begin to really get tough in shutting down that flow of funds.

The CHAIRMAN. Senator Flake.

Senator FLAKE. Thank you. Thank you, Mr. Secretary, for laying out the strategy. I think you know where this committee is and where I am in terms of wanting to give the President and the administration the authority and the wherewithal to move ahead and succeed in this mission and all our foreign policy missions.

But I am a little confused at the position that is being taken by the administration now that AUMF is not required, would be desired, but not required now. I look back at one of the last hearings that you appeared in. It was with regard to Syria and chemical weapons. The President, as you know, had drawn a redline and said that he would act if they went beyond it. They went beyond it, and then the President came to Congress and said what do you want me to do.

I questioned whether or not that was a wise move. And you said to me—these are your words—''It is somewhat surprising to me that a member of Congress, particularly one on the Foreign Relations Committee, is going to question the President for fulfilling the vision of the Founding Fathers when they wrote the Constitution, divided power in foreign policy, to have the President come over here and honor the original intent of the Founding Fathers in ways that do not do anything to distract from the mission itself.''

Now, I would argue, and I think others would as well, that that did distract from the mission itself. In fact, it torpedoed it, coming to Congress when we said we were going to strike and what was described as a 10-day or 2-week mission to degrade the ability to use chemical weapons. But then in this case, in what you, yourself, today describe as what will be a multiyear effort, say that you do not need—you desire, but do not need congressional buy-in.

It is best when we speak with one voice. Our allies know that. And in order to build the kind of coalition that is going to be required to, one, defeat ISIL, and, two, sustain that defeat over time, our coalition partners and our adversaries have to believe our threats and our promises. And I would submit that it helps for us to be together. So I question the unwillingness to come and ask for a renewed AUMF. Can you enlighten me as to why the change of heart from the last hearing?

Secretary KERRY. There is no change of heart, Senator, honestly. There is a big difference between the authorities that are available. We did not have authority in any form sufficient without Congress passing it, except for Article 2—excuse me. We had Article 2 authority for the President of the United States, which is always there, and nobody has ever gotten to the question of whether or not he would have exercised it had Congress not passed it.

But the fact is the President did make a decision to strike. He made a decision and publicly announced it. He said, I have made a decision to strike. Then, as you know, there were a lot of requests in our briefings with Congress to come to Congress. And since we did not have authority beyond Article 2, and that is the distinction between then and now.

Then the 2001 AUMF did not cover chemical weapons with Assad. It covered terrorism and al-Qaeda. And so, if it were not ISIL that was this direct component of al-Qaeda, and we were talking about, for instance, one of the other entities there, we might not have the same capacity here. But we are looking at an entity that was al-Qaeda from 2004 or 2005 all the way through until 2013, and then tried to disassociate itself by name, but continued to do the very same things it was doing with al-Qaeda the entire time. That is not true of what happened with Assad.

Now, it also happened, and I remember this distinctly, obviously, that during the walk-up to the process of the request for the AUMF, President Putin and President Obama had a conversation in St. Petersburg regarding the removal of weapons. Prime Minister Netanyahu had called me, and we had talked about the possibility of removal of weapons.

Senator FLAKE. I have just got a few seconds here, but I appreciate that history. But I hope we have a better explanation than that when we go to our allies and say that we are going to be in it for the long haul, and that we are united in this mission.

Secretary KERRY. And that is why we want Congress to pass AUMF. And I think five times in the course of this hearing I have said we welcome the effort work with you to refine the AUMF going forward, and, yes, we will be stronger and better with the passage of an AUMF and with Congress involved in it. But we are not going to put ourselves in the position of not being able to do what we believe we need to do with legitimacy at this moment in time. But we welcome it.

Senator FLAKE. With respect, I would argue that is what we did to ourselves before. We put ourselves in a position where we drew a redline, and then were not willing to do what it takes to go and enforce that redline.

Secretary KERRY. Well, but——

Senator FLAKE. And that is going to affect our ability to move forward and build the kind of coalitions that we need to do this mission. And that is why I am saying I think there is an inconsistency here. I hope that the administration will change its mind and ask firmly for an AUMF, and I hope Congress gives it. With that, I yield back.

The CHAIRMAN. Senator Udall.

Senator UDALL. Thank you very much, Mr. Chairman. Secretary Kerry, thank you for your tireless, committed, caring approach to these international issues, all of the ones which are so pressing today. And I think you are probably one of the most traveled Secretaries we have ever had. And I think all of us wish you the very best in your endeavors.

Chairman Menendez, I would like to thank you for this hearing. I think it is very important that we carefully weigh the President's request. We must address the very real threat presented by ISIS. A little over a year ago, we were in this same room talking about air strikes on the Assad regime and arming rebels to fight it, and due to Assad's use of chemical weapons. Today Assad's weapons are gone, and thank you, Secretary Kerry, I think, for your diplomatic efforts there.

And we are debating now, air strikes on ISIS and arming rebels to fight that. That is really, in a way, quite a turnaround. The American people deserve a full debate and explanation about this new plan that you have presented. And we have heard today a number of Senators—ISIS—talk about this. ISIS is a brutal terrorist organization. It must be stopped. And that is a subject I think we can all agree on. And I would associate myself with all of the comments—the previous comments about their brutality and their murderous ways. I do think there is any doubt about that.

We have a clear responsibility to continue to work with local groups, with our allies in the region, and for as long as it takes. We must use strategic force, I believe, to stop ISIS and end its murderous path, but let me be clear here. I do not want us to lose sight of the forest from the trees. There are calls for more and more direct U.S. military intervention in the Middle East, putting us back on a very risky course.

ISIS has thrived on the chaos, on the instability, the unintended consequences of America's failed policy in Iraq for the past 13 years, and this is the crucial point. Military power is one tool, one among many tools, that will be needed to bring stability to the region. ISIS emerged from disorder, from dysfunction, and alienation, and the divide between Sunni and Shia followers of Islam. Those conditions will remain without a comprehensive strategy of diplomacy, development, and commitment to long-term stability.

We must destroy ISIS, but we cannot put ourselves in the situation of creating a void, one that could then be filled by other extremists or by an Iranian-controlled regime. We should support the Iraqi Government, as well as the Kurdish and other moderate forces. However, I remain skeptical about the so-called moderate forces. And, Secretary Kerry, you have heard several times here this issue about moderate forces and are there moderate forces.

And I think one of the key issues for us is the effectiveness of the moderate forces that are there on the ground now. And my question to you has to do with—and this all public information, and everybody is well aware there has been a covert operation operating in the region to train forces, moderate forces, to go into Syria and to be out there. We have been doing this the last 2 years.

And probably the most true measure of the effectiveness of moderate forces would be what has been the effectiveness over that last 2 years of this covert operation of training two to 3,000 of these moderates. Are they a growing force? Have they gained ground? How effective are they? What can you tell us about this effort that has gone on, and has it been a part of the success that you see that you are presenting this new plan on?

Secretary KERRY. Senator, I hate to do this, but I know it has been written about in the public domain that there is ''a covert operation,'' but I cannot confirm or deny whatever that has been written about it, and I cannot really go into any kind of possible program.

Senator UDALL. Okay. Well, I want to say to Chairman Menendez, I mean, to me, the key here on effectiveness is what has happened these past 2 years. And so, I think we should have a briefing by our committee specifically on what has gone on in that area from our intelligence people.

And just one final thing. ISIS is already in possession of U.S. weapons paid for by U.S. taxpayers that extremists seized from United States-trained Iraqi Forces and Syrian rebels. How will you guarantee or assure that the weapons and resources you are requesting now will now end up in the hands of radical Sunni insurgents?

Secretary KERRY. Well, we have been following that very, very closely, and our folks who have been involved in this at all levels. And, again, this probably ought to be in the classified session for various reasons. But what we have been doing is providing various kinds of support to them, nonlethal, as I think you know. And we are vetting people very, very carefully.

And our folks who do that, because this is something we have really watched very carefully. The President has been very concerned about this question of downstream and impact. There are a couple of instances of an overrun of a warehouse up in the north and Aleppo and one instance a couple of things. But by and large, we have found the vetting to be pretty effective. Our guys have been doing it for about 20 years now, you know, for better or worse, and they have gotten pretty good at it.

Senator UDALL. Thank you. And I would also agree with, and I appreciate your offer to work with us on an authorization of force.

I think we have to have one with what you are describing, and I hope that we can get to that as soon as possible. I yield back.

The CHAIRMAN. Senator Udall, let me take your request and say, first of all, we will have as robust intelligence briefings as we can. However, to the core question that you raise, this is a problem that both the administration as well as the Senate leadership must be willing to deal with because when it comes to questions of being briefed on covert operations, this committee does not have access to that information. Yet it is charged with the responsibility of determining whether or not the people of the United States should, through their representatives, support an authorization for the use of military force.

It is unfathomable to me to understand how this committee is going to get to those conclusions without understanding all of the elements of military engagement both overtly and covertly. And so, I am four square with you, but this is a challenge—I will call it for lack of a better term—a procedural hurdle that we are going to have to overcome if we want the information to make an informed judgment and to get members on board.

Before I turn to Senator McCain, let me just recognize some distinguished members of the Kurdish delegation and the Iraqi Ambassador, Lukman Faily. I appreciate your being here. And in the Kurdish delegation, the chief of staff to President Barzani, Fuad Hussein, as well as the Minister of Foreign Affairs for the Kurdistan regional government, Falah Bakir. So thank you both for being here.

Senator McCain.

Senator McCAIN. Thank you, Mr. Chairman. I also want to recognize our Kurdish friends who have been such steadfast and good allies for so long.

Mr. Secretary, today, September 17, Secretary Gates said the following—former Secretary of Defense Gates. ''The reality is they are not going to be able to be successful against ISIS strictly from the air or strictly depending on the Iraqi Forces or the Peshmerga or the Sunni tribes acting on their own.'' Gates said, ''So there will be boots on the ground if there is to be any hope of success in the strategy. And I think that by containing—by continuing to repeat that that the U.S. will not put boots on the ground, the President, in effect, traps himself.''

Now, Mr. Secretary, I have talked to so many people who are military experienced, who have been on both sides on this issue. They all agree with Secretary Gates' assessment, and that is just the reality. And there are some of us that place a great deal of confidence in the opinion of people like Secretary Gates, General Keane, the architects of the surge, so many others. Now, is it your view that the Syrian opposition is viable? Hello?

Secretary KERRY. Hello, Senator. I am taking you so seriously I am writing notes.

Senator McCAIN. Is it your view the Syrian opposition is viable?

Secretary KERRY. The Syrian opposition has been viable enough to be able to survive under difficult circumstances——

Senator McCAIN. Are you——

Secretary KERRY [continuing]. But not yet—but they still have some distance to go, and we need to help them go that distance.

Senator MCCAIN. Right. And they obviously need our assistance in weapons and training, which you are going to embark on. Are you surprised sometimes at the degree of disinformation that Members of Congress will swallow whole, like there has been a ceasefire agreement between the Free Syrian Army and ISIS put out by ISIS? Does that surprise you sometimes?

Secretary KERRY. Senator, sometimes.

Senator MCCAIN. No, it does not surprise you. It does not surprise you. I got it.

Secretary KERRY. No, no, no.

Senator MCCAIN. The hero of this piece so far in my view is a guy who is going to testify here after you, Robert Ford—Ambassador Ford. He did a magnificent job at the risk of his own life riding around Damascus in support of the Free Syrian Army. Now, here is what he is going to say in his testimony. ''The moderate armed opposition's biggest enemy is not the Islamic State. It is the Assad regime, which has killed far more Syrians than has the detestable Islamic State. And they will not stop fighting the Assad regime even as they advance against the Islamic State.''

But you are saying ISIL first. So we are going to train and equip the Free Syrian Army, and they are going to be fighting against Assad, who they view as their number one enemy. I agree with Ambassador Ford's assessment, but you are saying ISIL first.

So if this—so we are telling a young Syrian today, I want you to join the Free Syrian Army. You go to fight ISIL first. And, by the way, those barrel bombs that are being dropped on you and these attacks from the air that have massacred so many Syrians, we are not going to do anything about that. I think at least we owe the Free Syrian Army to negate the air attacks that they will be subjected to when they finish their training and equipping, and go into the fight.

So why is it that we will not at least neutralize Bashir Assad's air activity, which has slaughtered thousands and thousands and thousands—192,000 dead, 3 million refugees? And we are not going to do anything about Assad's air capabilities?

And finally, ISIL first, that is what you are telling these young men who really view Assad as the one who has slaughtered their family members, not ISIL, as bad as ISIL is. So how do you square that circle, Mr. Secretary?

Secretary KERRY. Well, you square it this way, Senator. And, first of all, let me just say a word. I think everybody knows I had the pleasure of working with Robert Ford in the Department from the day I arrived there.

Senator MCCAIN. We share admiration for him, yes.

Secretary KERRY. And we worked very closely together. I have huge respect and admiration for him. And he and I worked many long hours with the Syrian opposition, and I respect his opinion, et cetera. He is correct that they will not stop fighting the Assad regime. I understand that. We understand.

Senator MCCAIN. They not only will not stop fighting, it is their primary goal.

Secretary KERRY. Well, it is except that——

Senator MCCAIN. I know too many of them, John. Go ahead.

Secretary KERRY. I understand. It is. I am not denying that. But they also are fighting ISIL. They are up in Aleppo right now fighting ISIL. They are fighting ISIL in other places. They threw them out of Idlib province. They are engaged in fighting ISIL. And our belief is, I think—I bet you—I hope Robert Ford believes that they will actually get stronger as a result of ISIL being removed from the field.

Senator MCCAIN. Are you not going to protect them from air strikes?

Secretary KERRY. I think what we need—yes. And I think what we need—that is a legitimate concern, and it is a concern that I would need to address with you in a classified session for reasons I think you well understand, and I think Robert Ford well understands that.

Senator MCCAIN. I think the Free Syrian Army would like to understand, too.

Secretary KERRY. And if we have a good classified session and other good things happen, who knows. The important thing is for us to recognize that if ISIL continues doing what it is doing, and I think you know this, without being stopped, and if we had not stood up when we did stand up and work with the Peshmerga and help them to push back and retake Mosul Dam and so forth—they were threatening Baghdad, and they were threatening more. And if they did that sufficiently——

Senator MCCAIN. John, we are talking about Syria and——

Secretary KERRY. No, I know, but I am about to come back.

Senator MCCAIN [continuing]. The Free Syrian Army.

Secretary KERRY. I am about to come because that——

Senator MCCAIN. Thank you. Thank you. I am running out of time.

Secretary KERRY. That pertains to their capacity then to focus on Assad, and it might be not the Free Syrian Army, but ISIL that you see in Damascus, and ISIL bringing al-Nusra and other people to them because of the level of their success. Clearly many people have told us in the region success breeds success, and many of the people who have come to ISIL have come because it seems as if they were not being opposed. Well, we believe that transition works to the benefit of the moderate opposition, works ultimately to all of our benefit by removing ISIL from the field.

Senator MCCAIN. You cannot ask people to go and fight and die unless you promise them that we will defeat their enemy and defeat them right away. You cannot say wait until we defeat ISIL. People will not volunteer for such things.

Secretary KERRY. I do not believe that is going to be ultimately a wait and see because I do not believe, number one, that the people supporting the opposition in various parts of the region are ever going to stop until the Assad problem is resolved. And number two, I do not believe ISIL is going to—I do not believe that the moderate opposition will obviously stop in that effort. So, therefore, there will be these two prongs. There is no way to avoid that.

Senator MCCAIN. I hope there are two prongs and not ISIL first, that that message is not given to these brave young people who we are asking to sacrifice——

Secretary KERRY. Well, if we do not stop ISIL first, there may not be much left of the other prong.

Senator MCCAIN. John——

The CHAIRMAN. Senator Murphy.

Senator MCCAIN. That means we cannot take on two adversaries at once.

Secretary KERRY. It is not us.

Senator MCCAIN. That is bogus and false.

The CHAIRMAN. I know you two colleagues would like to go at it for the rest of the session, but——

Secretary KERRY. No, no, no. [Laughter.]

The CHAIRMAN. We have other—I am sorry.

Secretary KERRY. We have a great tradition. I believe in John's adage that a fight not joined is a fight not enjoyed. So we always have a great time.

The CHAIRMAN. Senator Coons. I am sorry.

Senator COONS. Thank you, Chairman Menendez, and thank you, Secretary Kerry, for appearing, and for outlining, and for discussing with us in detail the strategy to degrade and destroy ISIL. And, I, too, want to thank Ambassador Ford for his commendable service and his ongoing commitment to the people of Syria.

I share your grave concern about ISIL, the threat it poses to our regional allies and to the United States, and the actions that they took in the massacring of Christians, Yazidis, Turkoman. And I am proud that we have stood up to them, and I am eager to hear and learn more about the strategy and exactly how it will play out.

First, Mr. Secretary, if I might, in your visit to Baghdad last week, the Prime Minister announced a proposal to establish a national guard style force of Sunnis that would reclaim and protect predominantly Sunni areas. And I think reconciliation between Shia and Sunni in the formal government and in the underground conditions in Iraq is absolutely essential to our having a prospect of success.

Can you explain how long it will take to establish this national guard style Sunni force on the ground in Iraq, how this model will work, and if there would be any role for our National Guard in training or equipping or supporting this Iraqi national guard?

Secretary KERRY. Senator Coons, that is a really good question, and I do not have all those answers at this point in time. I mean, there are military decisions with respect to who is going to be involved in training them and whether there is room for some National Guard input, et cetera. I am confident that the military folks would not dream of advising and assisting with respect to the National Guard structure without using their experience within our military as to how it has worked here and how it has been effective.

Senator COONS. Then let me ask a related question.

Secretary KERRY. That said—but that said, let me just say very quickly. The theory of it is to try to localize capacity in a way, as I think you know, that deals with this sectarian divide. One of the reason that the "Iraq army," as it has been called, folded in Mosul and before the wave of ISIL was frankly that the—some of the officers abandoned the men who were left behind. And there was a real sense of sectarian divide there.

Senator COONS. Right.

Secretary KERRY. They left because they were perceived by many people, and this was part of the problem with Iraq at that time, that there was a Sunni—there was a Sunni-Shia divide, sectarian divide within the construct of the military itself. And people to some degree felt even that it went so far as to be the prime minister's personal military entity, and there was not a stake in it.

So it was the absence of that commitment that motivated people to take off, and that has to be done away with, and there has be a unity. So whatever this national guard is, it is going to have to still be unified and connected to the state to ensure a sense of national enterprise, but made up of people who are—have a greater stake in their local community in their region, which was absent previously.

Senator COONS. I strongly agree and support your hard work on the diplomacy side of trying to address the challenges in Iraq, because if we have a Shia-only government and military, it is not sustainable, and that is in some ways what created the vacuum.

Let me move on to two regional questions, if I could. Has the campaign against ISIL affected our ongoing negotiations to end Iran's illicit nuclear program? And how has a potentially expanded military campaign against ISIL made it more difficult to find a final deal between Iran and the P5+1, the deadline coming in November, or have the mutual interests of Iraq and some of the P5+1 members provided a common point of interest for ongoing dialogue? How has it affected our——

Secretary KERRY. Well, we hope it is going to be the latter. We hope obviously very much it will be the latter part of your question that it has not affected it, that it can continue. Our P5+1 folks left for New York this afternoon. We will be engaging in that activity over the course of the next days, and we will get a better sense of it.

My belief is that the nuclear issue is so huge in its consequences, not just to Iran, but to the region, to the world, to all of us, the interest in getting rid of the sanctions, which is the end goal here with respect to Iran and our end goal of being able to reach an agreement is significant enough. And to the credit of people in the P5+1, thus far there has been a compartmentalization. Russia and China are both very constructively continuing to be active and involved in the negotiations and constructive with them. And our hope is that that will prevail going forward, but the answer is not yet defined fully.

Senator COONS. Let me make sure you are not misunderstood because I do not think you meant exactly what you just said. The end goal is not to end the sanctions. The end goal is not to reach——

Secretary KERRY. The end goal is to end the nuclear possibility, but what I said is their end—I think I said their end goal.

Senator COONS. I thought that might be a helpful clarification.

Secretary KERRY. No, no, no. I said there—I thought I said their desire is to obviously get the sanctions. You cannot do that—you cannot lift the sanctions without absolutely guaranteeing that the four pathways to a nuclear weapon have been closed off. And that is what we are working at.

Senator COONS. Last question. I am very concerned about the stability, security, safety of the Hashemite Kingdom of Jordan, our vital ally in the region, which has borne so much of the challenge and the burden of the refugees from Syria. And I am concerned that ISIL has had efforts to infiltrate Jordan, and there have been some isolated outbreaks of violence in Jordan related to ISIL. What are we doing and what more can we do to strengthen King Abdullah and to partner with him and work with him as we expand the mission we are talking about here as it has some impact, not just in Syria and Iraq, but also in Jordan?

Secretary KERRY. Well, we are working very, very closely with our friends in Jordan. And I was in Jordan, and I met with King Abdullah a few days ago—last week, I think Wednesday night after I had been to Iraq. We spent the evening talking about the various things we need to do together. They are determined to be helpful to us, and we are determined to be helpful to them, and we will be.

We are committing additional funds. We are committing additional equipment and capacity. And, you know, everybody shares concerns with all the neighbors in the region. I mean, ISIL—that is one of the reasons why this is so critical. And I can assure that you that an already extremely robust mil-to-mil, intel-to-intel and, you know, supply assistance program and economic program will be even more robust going forward. And you all have the budget, and you know what we are trying to do.

Senator COONS. Thank you, Mr. Secretary.

The CHAIRMAN. Senator Barrasso.

Senator BARRASSO. Thank you, Mr. Chairman. Mr. Secretary, thank you very much for coming. Yesterday's New York Times headline, "Kerry Says U.S. is Open to Talking to Iran." And you just—and I agree with your comments about the nuclear issue is so huge. You do talk about compartmentalization and also that Iran's goal is to eliminate the sanctions.

We have already seen the administration roll back sanctions—January, $7 billion in sanction relief. The administration recently introduced and announced another $2.8 billion in Iran sanction release. There are serious concerns that the administration could further relieve and remove sanctions in terms of trying to get concessions relating to Iran and the fight in Syria or Iraq. Clearly Iran and the United States do not have the same goals that we have in Syria, so I am curious, what are you hoping to achieve by reaching out to Iran regarding ISIL?

Secretary KERRY. Well, Senator, let me clarify something because it is very important to understand it. Every aspect of the interim agreement that we arrived at with Iran, which required Iran to do certain things, they have done, every aspect. And the5 thing that is outstanding still is the IAEA compliance where a recent meeting was not as forthcoming as people would have liked. But with respect to the agreement they entered into with the United States, they have done all the things they said they would do.

We have people daily inspecting in Fordow. Before that agreement, we had none. We have people daily inspecting Natanz. Before the agreement, we had none. We have people in Iraq on a periodic basis with the plans being delivered to us with the commissioning completely halted, and before that that was not true. I mean, I can run down a list.

We have had access to centrifuges, centrifuge production, centrifuge storage. We have mining and milling and, you know, a clarity here as to their activities that simply did not exist. That is what we have gotten out of this. Their program has been halted where it was when we began. And they have reduced their stockpile of 20 percent going down to zero. That is an extraordinary thing. For all the people who frankly said to us it is never going to work, the sanctions will come apart, that is not what has happened. The sanctions regime has not only held, there have been additional sanctions.

Now, yes, was there an agreement to release a portion of an initial round of some of the money that had been escrowed and held? Yes, $4.6 billion. Was there an agreement for the extension of a plan that continued this cooperation of $2.8? Yes. That is a total of about, what, $7 billion over, what, 9 months or something. The fact is that during that same amount of time, tens of billions of dollars have been withheld. There is more than a hundred—I forget the exact figures—more than a hundred and some billion that Iran believes it has a right to and wants that is being held in a freeze account until this gets resolved.

So I would have to say to you, Senator, this has been an enormous success thus far. Our hope is that in exchange for whatever schedule might be worked out, all of which will have to be subject to public scrutiny and a final agreement, any pathway to a bomb will be eliminated with a sufficient breakout time that we have the ability to come to you and say the world is safer, our allies in the region are safer, and this is a deal that people believe can be upheld. That is the goal.

We are not there yet. I do not know if we can get there. I hope we can get there because the alternatives are, you know, more complicated.

Senator BARRASSO. I do not want to get to a point where the sanctions have been removed and they are still on a path to producing a bomb.

Secretary KERRY. That will not happen.

Senator BARRASSO. Switching a little bit to follow up with Senator McCain, do we have any intelligence on how the Assad regime is going to react should the coalition launch airstrikes on ISIS targets in Syria in terms of commitments that Assad will not intervene specifically? We know ISIS does not have the capability to shoot down our jet bombers, but Syria does. And are there precautions in place to prevent that?

Secretary KERRY. The answer is, Senator, we are going to take precautions, but what I need to do is take it up with you in a classified session.

Senator BARRASSO. A couple of final questions on hostages. Do you know how many American hostages we believe are being held by ISIS or militant groups right now?

Secretary KERRY. Somewhere about three or four. I do not want to get—I think we have got to be careful on the numbers.

Senator BARRASSO. The concern is that, you know, after the barbaric murder of James Foley, the operational details of rescue attempts were leaked to the press, including the special operations unit. And I just wanted to make sure that the administration is committed to working to stop leaking classified information that undermines our military operations.

Secretary KERRY. I honestly do not know where it came from. I cannot tell you that. We have a problem in this city with leaks in every department of government. And we try, believe me, to stop that.

Senator BARRASSO. Thank you, Mr. Chairman.

The CHAIRMAN. Senator Murphy.

Senator MURPHY. Thank you very much, Mr. Chairman. The world today is more complicated, more dangerous than at any time during our lifetimes. And I wake up every day thankful that we have leaders like you and President Obama, thoughtful, strategic, guiding our way through it. So thank you for all the work that you are doing and for enduring this process for as long as you have.

It strikes me that we are dealing with a fundamentally new problem in a frustratingly familiar context. The new problem is ISIL. They are on the verge of becoming the world's first autonomous terrorist state if they are successful. I have no doubt that they will turn their focus on the United States and our allies. But the familiar new problem is the Middle East, and if we have learned anything over the last 12 years of war it is that the Middle East seems largely immune from U.S. efforts to bend it to our will.

And so, that is not an excuse to idly by. It is just a reason why we have to be very careful about crafting a strategy that is not just well intentioned, but realistic. And so, I think that you and the President have got it largely right. I think I am broadly supportive of the strategy that you have laid with one exception, and so I want to just bring us back to the question about arming and trading with Syrian rebels.

When we talked about this in open session a year ago, we raised concerns about the potential for the Free Syrian Army to coordinate with the al-Nusra wing of al-Qaeda, and there was confidence that that would not end up being the case. But we have a variety of reports that that indeed has been the practice, most recently in a joint effort between the Free Syrian Army and al-Nusra fronts to take a border post between Syria and Israel.

So let me ask you that question. You answered Senator Udall's question about the ways in which we can keep arms from flowing to Islamic extremist groups. But why are you confident—how can you give us confidence that we are not going to train a fighting force that is then going to enter a battle with a known affiliate of al-Qaeda? And how confident are we that ultimately when they get on the field of battle that they are not going to look to ISIS, who is fighting the same enemy that they originally entered into battle against, Assad, in common cause?

Secretary KERRY. Well, Senator, there is no fail-safe obviously. As I said earlier in answer to an earlier question, our guys have gotten much, much better at the vetting. And now that we are doing the training to some degree and hopefully do it openly, we are going to be in a much better position to do command and control, to do, you know, much greater in-depth accountability, if you will.

In the end, there probably will be some strange bedfellow moments in the course of this kind of battle. I would be crazy if I sat here and just said to you, oh, it will never happen, there is nobody—you know. There are exigencies and circumstances that we do not always control. But by and large, we are beginning to get a much better handle with other players in the region on the funding streams, for instance, to al-Nusra.

Different countries that have played the angles with certain groups are now coalescing together. And we see a shift, and I think that is going to be to our benefit to be able to exercise at least a greater amount of control. Fail-safe, I cannot sit here and promise you that, but we are going to do the best we can.

Now, let me just say to you—all of you here a couple of things. One, the House just passed the Syria Train and Assist and Equip bill, and obviously we hope the House having done that, that the Senate will follow suit in short order. I also want to just correct one thing I said earlier. I was talking about the JPOA, the agreement, and John is gone. But I just want to emphasize, I did not mean to say we did not have any inspection before. We did not have daily inspection. We had some inspection through our process, but now we have the daily, and we did not have a sufficient level to have guarantees in a place like Fordow that we have a comfort level.

One other thing can I just say because you raised this, Senator Murphy?

Senator MURPHY. It is fine.

Secretary KERRY. Okay.

Senator MURPHY. Go ahead.

Secretary KERRY. No, go ahead. I will answer it following your question.

Senator MURPHY. Well, here is my—I guess my only followup is this. I understand that there are going to be strange bedfellows, but to the extent that the strange bedfellows are the Free Syrian Army fighting alongside al-Nusra, which is a wing and affiliate of al Qaeda, I hope that is not a reality that we are prepared to accept. We have had all sorts of talk about ISIL, but it is important to remember that the only major terrorist organization that has plans and stated intentions to carry them out against the United States today is al Qaeda. So I just want to make sure that we have a specific focus on that particular set of strange bedfellows.

Secretary KERRY. I am with you 100 percent, and we will to the greatest degree possible, absolutely. But what I wanted to say to everybody here is you mentioned something very important a moment ago, which was about ISIL being a terrorist state and so forth. This is one of the things that I ran into very strongly with all the meetings I had in the region. And I want to just share with you this, that one of the key parts of this strategy is to not ever give them the legitimacy that they are trying to seek as to being a state. They have no legitimacy. They are not an Islamic state, and they are not in the vein of any other state in that region that tries to give meaning to the concept of Islamism as they celebrate it with their citizens and their countries.

And this is important for us because, you know, Islam does not produce—no legitimacy in Islam produces the butchers who killed

Steven Sotoloff or David Haines or, you know, Jim Foley. That is not Islam, and Islam is not ISIL. And increasingly all of the voices in the region are really starting to feel that they have a need to speak out and to reclaim Islam, and that is one of the most important things that could come out of this. And we are working on ways to do that.

So ISIL is not a state obviously. It is not remotely like a state, and what we need to do is make that more clear. So let me just share with you two important things. The Grand Mufti of Saudi Arabia, the home of Mecca and Medina, which, by the way, are in the target scale of ISIS, these are Islam's most holy cities, they said of these murderers they are enemy number one of Islam. That comes from the Grand Mufti of Saudi Arabia.

And today, Saudi Arabia's top clerical council, all 21 members, the only institution in the Kingdom of Saudi Arabia that is authorized to issue fatwahs, invoking Muhammad, using the words of the Koran itself, today they said that ISIL are killers. They are thugs. They should be singled out and punished as apostates under Sharia, and made an example of. And they said they were not following the Prophet, but that these—and these are their words, not mine. They are following the order of Satan.

Now, that is what you are beginning to hear from the region, and that is a key part of this strategy. And obviously we do not have the legitimacy to do what people in the region can do to de-legitimize, but we are certainly going to do everything in our power to help encourage that and make sure that people are aware of it.

The CHAIRMAN. Senator Paul.

Senator PAUL. Thank you, and thank you for your testimony. I agree with you and with the President that we must confront and destroy ISIL. I think that, you know, I am well on record as being very skeptical about our interventions in the Middle East. I think that the original war in Iraq has led to more chaos and less stability. I think the President's war in Libya as well as your intervention in Syria have led to less stability and more radical Islam throughout the country, and have actually enabled ISIL.

I do also and have been a frequent critic of Secretary Clinton for not providing adequate security, though, for Benghazi and for the consulate. So I do think that there is an American interest in defending our Embassy in Baghdad as well as our consulate in Erbil. And I want there to be some message going forward from this hearing today that there is obviously bipartisan support for defending American interests in Iraq.

However, I am very disappointed, though, in the President for not obeying the Constitution. The Constitution is very clear. It gave the power to declare war to Congress. And you can say, hey, we are going to come back when it is convenient, but we are going to be committing war for the next 3 or 4 months, and we will do as we please. That is not what the Constitution intended.

The interesting thing about the creative logic that used to say that a vote in 2001 has anything to do with today is that it seems to be acknowledged that, well, that allows you to do anything with forces that may be associated with terrorism or al-Qaeda. One of the interesting things is if you look at Ambassador Ford's testimony, he will say that ''Moderate forces have and will tactically coordinate with al-Qaeda, with al-Qaeda linked to al-Nusra.'' So the interesting thing, if we use your logic and say the 2001 AUMF can be used to justify this, well, the 2001 AUMF could be used to justify going after the moderate Syrian rebels who are associated with al-Qaeda.

So I think really anybody who is intellectually honest would say that the people who voted in 2001 to go to war with the people who attacked us on 9/11, the people who congregated in Afghanistan, has absolutely nothing to do with this. And really this committee, Congress, Senate, and the President are all abdicating the responsibility to vote for a new use of authorization of force, and that what you are doing now is illegal and unconstitutional.

I think also from a practical point of view, it would be better to bring the country together. I think we would galvanize more support. It would be a bipartisan war. And had the President been a great leader, he should have come before a joint Congress instead of going on TV. He should have come before a joint Congress and immediately asked for a resolution, and there should have been a vote. That would have been true leadership. There would have been true bipartisan support, and then really there would be less carping on both sides.

The President also used to believe this. The President ran, and it was one of the large reasons the public went for the President initially, is he said no President should unilaterally go to war without the authority of Congress. So I liked the President as a candidate on this issue, but not so much as the President.

The other problem with this is that, you know, who are these moderate people? Are there really moderate, you know, Islamic rebels in Syria? Here is a quote, and I would like your comment on this. Ryan Crocker, the distinguished former United States Ambassador to both Iraq and Syria, said, that ''The administration's knowledge about the non-ISIS opposition in Syria is that we need to do everything we can to figure out''—this is Crocker. ''We need to do everything we can to figure out who the non-ISIS opposition is because, frankly, we do not have a clue.''

You know, most of the weapons we have been giving to the moderate rebels, they are sort of at a stopping place. That is where they stopped briefly before ISIS takes the weapons. Some of these, the Syrian National Revolutionary Front have signed—have signed a cease-fire. Maybe not all of the vetted rebels are, but the Syrian Revolutionary Front has signed a cease-fire.

So really, I argue, and I would believe, and I would like to hear your comment. I think we have allowed there to be more of a safe haven for ISIL in giving weapons to the so-called moderate rebels because really that has taken pressure off them. It has kept Assad at bay. And I think, contrary to what others have said here, had we bombed Assad last year, ISIL would be in Damascus.

So I think we are lucky we did not bomb Assad last year, and that we should be very careful about arming any Islamic rebels in Syria because the weapons may not stay where they are intended, and they may have the unintended consequence of actually enabling ISIL. Your comments?

Secretary KERRY. Well, we are not planning to, nor do we want to, nor have we armed Islamic folks in Syria. The United States does not do that, and we have opposed it, and Robert Ford will tell you. And Robert Ford worked very hard to make sure that we were not doing that.

I also think it is good that you are going to hear from Robert Ford because he will give you about as good an analysis of who the non-ISIS opposition is, and he will break it down point for point because he did that for me on many occasions and articulated who they were and so forth. But he was also a passionate supporter of making certain that the moderate opposition got support. And he fought hard to get it more support than they did get, absolutely. So I think he should do that for you.

But let me just make it clear that the—I mean, I am glad that you can guarantee that there would be a vote if the President sent up here. I have got 60 nominees, some of whom have been waiting more than a year to get a vote up here. And the chair and the ranking member have been terrific in helping to try to break them out, but they cannot get a vote. So if you can tell the President you can absolutely guarantee a vote, I would be really amazed.

Senator PAUL. I find it unbelievable that if the President came before a joint session of Congress and asked for use of force, that he would not get a vote. I find it unthinkable. There is absolutely no way that you can imagine that he would not get a vote if he asked for it, so really, let us be honest. Politics are engaged here. People do not want to have a vote before the election. They are afraid of this vote. People are petrified, not of the enemy, but petrified of the electorate. That is why we are not having a vote.

Secretary KERRY. Well, let me answer the first part of your question so that we make it crystal clear why the President is doing what he is doing, because you are not insinuating. You are stating quite declaratively that the President has violated the Constitution. The President absolutely, clearly, by almost any legal standard that I can imagine is not violating the Constitution. He is upholding it. Article 2 gives the President the power to do what he is doing. He has lived by the War Powers Act. He has sent countless notices up to the Congress. And I think every legal analysis suggests that while you may not like it——

Senator PAUL. If Article 2 gives unlimited power, why come at all?

Secretary KERRY. Senator, let me just finish. Because he believes that the Congress ought to do this, and no one has——

Senator PAUL. But he does not believe he is bound.

Secretary KERRY. The President has the right as the President under Article 2 to defend this Nation and to take the steps necessary to do so. The War Powers Act declares the terms under which you do that, Senator. You know that. And he has lived absolutely within that constitutional prerogative.

Secondly, like it or not, and I can agree. I think you can find reasons to be uncomfortable. That does not mean it is not legal. And the chairman of this committee is appropriately going to try to recalibrate the AUMF, which we support entirely. We welcome the opportunity to have it recalibrated. It should be. But for the moment, the President believes we need to move now, and that is a full and appropriate exercise of constitutional power.

Senator PAUL. And for the record, that will be after the election.

The CHAIRMAN. Senator Kaine.

Senator KAINE. Thank you, Mr. Chairman, and Mr. Secretary for your testimony. It has been an illuminating back and forth. I also want to thank Ambassador Ford and Mr. Connable, the written testimony that you each prepared. Very instructive. I often walk away from hearings older, but not smarter. I am walking away from this one older and smarter, so thank you for that.

Mr. Chairman, I want to thank you for your comments at the beginning with respect to the authorization. A number of us feel like additional congressional authorization for the mission as described by the President is mandatory. Some of us do not feel that. But all of us, I think, on both sides of the dais believe it is advisable. And your commitment to crafting that in an appropriate way is notable and important.

I have introduced a draft, and others have as well, that we know will be forwarded to this committee as we look to try to put something together that is, in fact, bipartisan, and it should be. Based on the statements around the table, it should be.

An observation. Tomorrow in Portsmouth, VA, a container ship, the MV *Cape Ray*, is returning to the Commonwealth of Virginia. It is a merchant marine ship with merchant marines and DOD personnel, and it is the ship that has been in the Mediterranean involved in the complete destruction of the declared Syrian chemical weapons stockpile. That is a good news day tomorrow. And I think it is something that we ought to just contemplate as we are thinking about U.S. power, that there was a diplomatic breakthrough that led to the destruction of one of the largest chemical weapons stockpiles in the world. The United States played a critical role and this committee played a critical role.

The diplomatic breakthrough, a factor in that was the willingness to use military force. Diplomacy is important. Often you get a much better result if you are really willing to use military force. Some interpret what happened last year as the President stepped away from a redline. No, there was a redline. We will take action against you if you use chemical weapons. We were prepared to take military action. Had we taken military action, the best we were going to get from the mission as described was convincing the Assad regime not to use chemical weapons again. But we were not going to get their complete destruction.

Those chemical weapons still would have been out there, possibly to have been seized by ISIL or other elements. What we now have, because of a willingness to use military force as a factor, is the complete destruction of a stockpile that is widely viewed as a real positive, especially by neighbors in the region. So as we move forward, diplomacy is important. Credible military threat is important. Those things can work together.

Mr. Secretary, you talked a lot about this. We are very deeply concerned about the extent of the coalition, and we understand as it is still coming together, the purpose for the hearing today is not to describe every Nation and what their role is. But just to sort of put it on the table for you and others, it is incredibly important that this coalition not just be vast, but that it also be public at the appropriate point, and that the participation of Arab nations, nations in the region, be public. They have often been willing to support the United States playing the lead in a financial way where they have not wanted to be public in condemning atrocities within their own region.

I do not think the American public, and I do not think Congress, will support the United States policing a region that will not police itself. And so, it is critically important for the success of the mission and for the success of both of getting bipartisan support and supporting the American public that the coalition be vast, but especially with the nations that their participation not be, you know, we will help finance it, but we do not want to be public about it. They have to be full public partners for this mission to be successful.

In addition, the importance of their public participation is critical to the success of the mission on the ground because if this is a campaign of the West against ISIL or the United States against ISIL, in a bizarre way, we will potentially legitimize ISIL even more. But if it is, and you read the quotes earlier that are helpful, if it is a public campaign by leaders in the region, whether they be religious leaders or clerics and certainly nations against ISIL.

This is not about Islam. You are a profanation of Islam in what you are doing. So the more public that is, the more ISIL is de-legitimized, and the ultimate success of this mission is not just a military success, it is a de-legitimization strategy that will strip away the pretense that this is an organization that has anything to do with Islam and demonstrating to the public that they need to back away from it and condemn it. And so, that is why the coalition thing is so critical, and the public nature of the coalition is important. And if you just want to comment on that briefly, please.

Secretary KERRY. Well, no, Senator, look, you have said it, and I think I have said it in the course of the hearing. We completely understand that. We do not want this just to be—this is not just an American effort. That is one of the reasons why the President took the time to make sure that the Iraqi Government was in place, that we were going to build a coalition, that we took the time to do what was necessary because we all understand that no one is advantaged by this being perceived of as just an American effort, and it is not. There are many other countries. I mean, France helped, stepped up, and bringing people to Paris the other day for a larger conference, and Jeddah, Saudi Arabia hosted that meeting. And countries that had not sat at the table together for some period of time were at that table.

One of the things that people really have not, I think, sufficiently focused on in this story is the Iraqi story. I mean, Iraq was on the brink 2 months ago, and many people were talking about, oh, my god, is it going to break up? Can it hold together? What is going to happen? We worked very, very closely with Iraqis, and Iraqis led that effort, all of them, you know. The Sunni folks who had bitter feelings about what happened in the last years came together, picked a new speaker.

The Kurds, who had plenty of reasons to be mistrustful and not, you know, be certain of the future, came together and elected a new president. And that new president had the courage to choose somebody other than the current Prime Minister to say you try to form a government. That could have faltered. It did not. They came together, put together that new government, actually ratified the new Prime Minister. The new Prime Minister has been continuing to put the government together. His Foreign Minister was in Jeddah, was in Paris.

So, you know, this photograph I pointed out of a, you know, of a Kurd President, of a, you know, Saudi Arabian Foreign Minister of a Shia-Iraqi Foreign Minister, all together conferring about how they are going to deal with ISIL tells you the story of an amazing transformation that has taken place. And I think people need to recognize that that is a big step forward. Now, we have to build on it.

The second thing I would just say about the Cape Ray coming back, I want to thank your people. I wish you would extend the huge gratitude of the administration and of the world for this incredible job well done. And you are absolutely correct. The President announced he was going to strike. We had already been talking with the Russians and others about how to get the weapons out, and then the deal came together and took away the necessity for the President to make a judgment he still would have made, whether or not to strike under his constitutional power based on the announcement he made.

But clearly getting 100 percent of the declared weapons out—we still have some questions about a few other things. But 100 percent, 1,300 tons of weapons out completely and destroyed is the first time that has ever happened in a time of conflict in any part of the world.

And I will tell you, ask Prime Minister Netanyahu, ask people in the region, they will tell you they are safer. You have an X factor that has now been eliminated from this whole equation of what we may or may not do in Syria as a consequence of that action.

The CHAIRMAN. Senator Markey.

Senator MARKEY. Thank you, and thank you for the excellent job which you are doing, Mr. Secretary. Turkey—Turkey does not want to become part of our combat operations because ISIL has hostages from Turkey. But at the same time, Turkey has become the destination for the oil which has been captured by the ISIL army in both Iraq and in Syria. And it is upward of a million to $3 million a day, $300 million to a billion dollars in the course of a year. In fact, the smuggled oil has now become the lifeblood of the ISIL army.

So talk a little bit about Turkey and what our efforts are going to be to just shut this down, because without that money, they do not have the money to produce Hollywood-style videos. They do not have the money to pay their soldiers. They do not have the money to take care of these cities and towns that they are taking over. Talk about what we have to do with Turkey to just get them to shut this down.

Secretary KERRY. Well, Senator, it is a very, very relevant question and one that we are working on very hard obviously. We really do understand the sensitivities that Turkey has. I do not want to talk about it too much publicly, to be honest with you, because of that. I think we are better off having a classified conversation about this. But I have hopes that as we move forward here over time, that the current dynamic may be able to shift in a way that will help us deal with that a lot more.

Turkey understands the challenges, believe me, and we have had some very candid conversations about it. But Turkey will have to make its decisions in the days ahead, and we will see what happens.

Senator MARKEY. It is unconscionable that Turkey has become the principal source of funding for ISIL, and if we can shut that down, we do almost immeasurable damage to their ability to finance this war. And I just think we have to put Turkey right front and center and have the world say to them, they must stop it.

Let me move on. The language which is in the resolution says that one of the goals is to promote the conditions for a negotiated settlement to end the conflict in Syria. We will be voting on that. So experts are saying that it will take upwards of 3 years to resecure the border between Iraq and Syria. And experts are also saying that it will take up to 10 years to create the conditions on the ground in Syria to bring Assad to the table in order to, in fact, have a negotiated settlement.

So I would ask you talk about those two timelines that experts are talking realistically given the weakness of the Free Syrian Army, how long it will take to build them up, how long it will take for us to push the ISIL army out of Iraq. The American people, I think, want to know how long we are going to be engaged in this effort toward the end game.

Secretary KERRY. Well, let me talk macro in a sense here, Senator, if I can. First of all, I have read various accounts of summaries of various experts, some of whom are experts and some of whom are called experts. And there is only one expert right now that I am looking to, and that is Gen. John Allen. He has the responsibility here. He is putting together his team very rapidly. He is having meetings, and I will listen to him very carefully before I start pushing out timelines.

Now, that said, President Obama has already said it is going to take a number of years to do the broad-based effort that we are at. And when I say that, you know, I think you can do a lot to ISIL fairly quickly, and then you have a longer fight as you begin to really go into the, you know, full destruction and defeat mode, so to speak.

But I got to tell you, and this is something that I expect to be talking about more with this committee and with Congress over the course of the next months. The fight of our generation is a combined fight against the immediate challenge of radical, religious extremism and its exploitation in various parts of the world, and large, unemployed populations of young people without good governance surrounding them and without opportunity, without dignity, respect. And this is a challenge we face, all of us, and all countries that consider themselves, you know, developed, and near-developed, and civilized.

It is our challenge, and we need to figure out how we are going to do all the things we need to do. And this is part of what President Obama talked about when he went to West Point, and about the focus on counterterrorism, and the need to talk more as we go forward in the days ahead about exactly how we are going to fill out the full agenda of our country to be safe in the long term.

It is a big, long-term operation, and that part of it is going to take years. And the United States, I think it is clear, is going to have to help lead that effort, and that is going to require a different attitude about foreign policy and engagement than a lot of people have been willing to embrace. I look forward to that discussion very much, and we are doing our homework to be able to come to you with thoughtful ideas about how we can deal with it.

Senator MARKEY. Thank you, Mr. Secretary. We are very fortunate to have you as the person sitting in that seat. Thank you.

Secretary KERRY. Well, you are because you are now in my seat. [Laughter.]

The CHAIRMAN. The most fortunate of them all. Well, Mr. Secretary, thank you for your engagement here today. You became the Secretary of State at a time in which I have never seen in 22 years in the Congress such a confluence of challenges globally as they exist right now, the topic we have been discussing here for the last 3 hours: the challenge of ISIL, the Russian invasion in Ukraine, the challenges of Ebola in Africa, the reality of our continuing challenge with Iran and its search for nuclear weapons, and the list goes on and on. And your service comes at an extraordinarily important time, so we want to salute you.

I do want to make one or two final comments. Number one is this is going to be an issue in which more information and a steady flow of information and briefings will be critical to having the congressional understanding and the ultimate support for what I believe is our mutual mission to defeat ISIL. And I just want to say that on various occasions, you have legitimately said that we need to have some of these conversations in classified settings. I will say that I look forward and intend to hold those classified hearings, but I hope it is going to be as robust so that when we get into a classified hearing, we do not have to hear, well, I cannot talk about that in that context. That will be problematic.

Secondly, there have been many—I do not question anybody's intentions here. I believe that there are many legitimate questions, and there are certainly legitimate questions when we think about putting America's sons and daughters into harm's way. We are strongest in the national challenge that we face when we speak with one voice, as Democrats, Republicans, and Independents together as Americans. And it is that unity of purpose I think that will be critical—a critical element of our success against ISIL. This is a moment in which politics must stop at the water's edge.

This committee for the last 2 years has taken on a whole host of major foreign policy and national security challenges in a bipartisan way, and I look forward to working with my colleagues to come together again to do that in this most critical case. I think we can.

And finally, I remind those who are concerned about the use of U.S. military might in a foreign country, that we face the world as it is, not as we wish it to be. I do not know how you negotiate with an entity that beheads Americans.

So thank you, Mr. Secretary, for your testimony and engagement for what I expect will be a continuing engagement. And before you have a parting word, I do want to urge colleagues, we have an important panel coming up with a lot of information, and I hope members will be able to stay or come back.

Mr. Secretary.

Secretary KERRY. I will be very, very brief. Just thank you very much. I look forward to having those discussions. And one coda, I think you know this. I long believed as chairman that the chairman and ranking member should have the same input as the chair and ranking member of the other committees—Armed Services, et cetera, Intel—because of the policy considerations. And I have advocated for that within this administration, and it is something that I think ought to happen.

The CHAIRMAN. Thank you. Thank you, Mr. Secretary.

Secretary KERRY. Thank you.

The CHAIRMAN. We appreciate your testimony. Let me call up our second panel today as the Secretary leaves. And I——

[Disturbance in hearing room.]

The CHAIRMAN. The committee will come to order. I will ask the Capital Police to remove individuals who will not come to order.

Our second panel today is Robert Ford, senior fellow of the Middle East Institute. And Ambassador Ford, of course, has a long and distinguished history in the Foreign Service of the United States, which he did so exceptionally well in Syria. And Ben Connable, the senior international policy analyst at the RAND Corporation here in Washington. I appreciate both of you. Both of your written statements will be included in the record in its entirety without objection.

And I appreciate your willingness to hang in there for the last several hours and to still be here to provide what I think is some critical testimony and insights. So with the thanks of the committee to both of you, I will recommend—I mean, I will recognize Senator—I mean, I will recognize Ambassador Ford first, and then we will turn to Mr. Connable.

Ambassador Ford.

STATEMENT OF HON. ROBERT S. FORD, SENIOR FELLOW, MIDDLE EAST INSTITUTE, WASHINGTON, DC

Ambassador FORD. Mr. Chairman, Senator Johnson, and other distinguished guests and members of the committee. It is a very big honor to be with you today, and I thank you for the invitation. And as you noted, I submitted a written statement. And so, let me just make a few opening remarks, and then I will turn it over to my copanelist, Ben.

Many have spoken about the dangers of the Islamic State against us and against our allies in the region. And I would simply note that I have been looking on Arabic social media sites in Arabic language, and some of the language is blood-curdling, the threats against us. And I take these people at their word, and they do present a serious danger to us.

The administration's proposal to increase assistance to moderate elements of the armed opposition in Syria will be useful as one part of addressing the Islamic State threat, and the administration's proposal deserves congressional support. I understand from you——

well, Secretary Kerry that the House has voted, and I hope the Senate does as well as soon as possible.

Let me just make three points. First, and I heard it again today here. People question whether there is a moderate armed opposition, but there is, and it is already fighting the Islamic State. I put some details about some of the groups in my written testimony, Mr. Chairman. When I say "moderate," what I mean by that word is that its leaders—the leaders of these groups do not seek to impose a religious state on Syrian society by force. Many of them are Islamists, Mr. Chairman, but they do not seek to impose a religious state by force.

That said, there are no angels in the Syrian war now. However, the moderate groups emanate from what were peaceful protest movements around Syria in 2011. These were the protest movements that I myself saw. And their leaders accept the idea that there has to be an eventual political deal in Syria. That also makes them moderate. Some of these groups, in fact, including groups in my written testimony, had representatives at the talks in Geneva where Secretary Kerry was present.

My second point is these moderates now are fighting the Islamic State. They lost badly in eastern Syria. They lost very badly. That is how the Islamic State took control of oil fields. They are holding their own right now in northern Syria not far from the Turkish border, but it is a hard fight. It is a desperate fight, and they would definitely benefit from greater and more reliable material aid in those battles against the Islamic State in northern Syria.

We just had a delegation here from the Iraqi Kurdish Government. Like the Iraqi Kurdish Peshmerga who are fighting the Islamic State on the Iraq side of the border, the moderate armed opposition in Syria would benefit as well from American airstrikes against Islamic state targets. And they would benefit more than Assad because those airstrikes up in northern Syria would help the moderates we are trying to help secure the moderates' vital supply lines. Assad does not even have forces that far north in Syria anyway.

My last point is that we have to go into this with our eyes open. The moderates in the Free Syrian Army and the Syrian armed opposition, their primary enemy is indeed still the Assad regime, which has killed far more Syrians than has the Islamic State, as awful and terrible as the Islamic State is. And so, as we try to work with them, they will always be thinking about how to manage their two-front war—the Islamic State on one side, the Assad regime on the other.

But as their resources from the entire coalition of countries that Secretary Kerry and the administration is assembling, as their total resources increase, they will have more resources to devote against the Islamic State, but I doubt that all of their new resources from all of the countries are going to be used only against the Islamic State. I think we have to understand that going in.

Mr. Chairman, I will be happy to take questions later, and thank you again for your invitation.

[The prepared statement of Ambassador Ford follows:]

PREPARED STATEMENT OF ROBERT S. FORD

Mr. Chairman, Senator Corker, members of the committee, it is an honor to be invited to speak with you today about what we should do in the face of a growing threat from the Islamic State.

I spent almost 5 years working within Baghdad as the senior political advisor and later deputy to Ambassadors John Negroponte, Zalmay Khalilzad, Ryan Crocker, and finally Chris Hill. I left Iraq in 2010.

And I then served on the ground in Damascus for a year before we had to close the Embassy in February 2012 and I returned home to head, for 2 years, the State Department team working on the Syria crisis.

It's been a grim 3 years, but I see some positive signs in Iraq that suggest guideposts as we think about next steps in Syria.

These signs result from policy approaches to contain and reduce extremist groups that also worked when I was in Iraq years ago.

Over the past several months in Iraq we identified groups on the ground in Iraq that rejected the Islamic State and that were sturdy enough to build upon.

The Iraqi Kurdish Peshmerga were not extremely well organized in June 2014—they had multiple command chains and there was confusion at the time of the fall of Mosul. And to be clear, the political goal of an independent Kurdistan shared by many Kurds is not one that the U.S. Government has endorsed.

Still, the Peshmerga represented a reliable core group that could use our help to confront the Islamic State's fighters on the ground.

And despite the collapse of many Iraqi army units, there were reliable special operations army units that again could usefully utilize our help to fight the Islamic State.

These Peshmerga and Iraqi Special Operations Forces together with a limited, judicious use of airstrikes pushed Islamic State fighters away from the Mosul Dam, from Erbil and Kirku parts of Diyala province.

The fight is not at all over, but the Islamic State's advance in Iraq has been blunted.

It's going to be a long fight.

The President, very wisely in my opinion, insisted that we could not fight the Iraqi battle against the Islamic State for them, however. He conditioned big American help on the Iraqis finding a political deal to set up a new government—a sort of unity government—that could rally all Iraqis to fight the Islamic State.

The President rightly understands that it is vital to undercut extremist recruiting among the disaffected Sunni Arab population by means of Iraqi political leaders figuring out a political deal.

I am very encouraged that various tribal figures in Anbar and Hawija, elected provincial councils in Mosul and Salah ad-Din all have come forward to offer to mobilize Sunni Arab fighters against the Islamic State if the new government in Baghdad will join with them. The initial statements I have seen from the new Prime Minister are also encouraging.

The regional states pledging to act with us in Iraq is also encouraging—and something we didn't really have when I was in Iraq years ago. Just the symbolism of the Iraqi Foreign Minister—a senior Shia politician—appearing in Riyadh at Saudi invitation with other Sunni states' representatives was very positive. We're in a better spot in this regard than we were in 2003 or 2007.

But as I said, if there are encouraging signs, we also need to understand that just as it took years to contain and reduce Al Qaeda in Iraq, so it will take years again in Iraq. Patience and firm insistence on our political conditions are vital.

Turning to Syria, it's a much harder problem than Iraq and we are long past the chance to find easy answers or sure bets. Still, the same elements used in Iraq offer the best path forward:

- We need to identify friendly forces on the ground and boost their ability to fight the Islamic State;
- We may need to use, judiciously, our own airpower;
- As in Iraq the real fighting will be on the ground, so equipment, ammunition, logistics, and even cash matter just as much if not more;
- A sustainable solution requires a new Syrian government via negotiations between Syrians with outside encouragement.

Many Americans question whether there are any moderates left in the Syrian armed opposition. There are. They are fighting the Islamic State and the Assad regime both, they are, not surprisingly, hard pressed, and they could very much use our help.

I find it odd that the media don't talk about them much. Units like the Hazem Brigade fighting in northwestern Syria that actually helped expel the Islamic State out of that part of Syria last spring. The Hazem Brigade issued a manifesto last March saying it was fighting for a pluralistic Syria where minorities' rights would be protected. Or units like the 101st and 13th divisions, fighting in both northern and southern Syria, led by former Syrian military officers. Or units like the Omari and Yarmouk brigades which are fighting regime forces in southern Syria. There are others too, of course.

Right now, some of these units, and others are locked in battle with the Islamic State near Aleppo in northern Syria.It's a hard fight—U.S. equipment the Islamic State captured from the Iraqi Army is being used against those Free Syrian Army fighters. However, these units also have received help from outside and they have fought the Islamic State to a standstill in that part of Syria. It's a desperate fight—the Islamic State is trying to capture vital supply lines for the moderate armed opposition coming down from Turkey.

Helping those units, right now, around Aleppo could secure supply routes and boost the morale of the moderate fighters. Assad's forces are some distance away and far too stretched already to hold ground northeast of Aleppo. Thus, we and our friends ramping up help there would not benefit Assad nearly as much as the moderate opposition.

We do need multiple changes in approach. Larger, more reliable logistics help, including provision of ammunition and cash, are a must if we hope to make any headway against the Islamic State. And just as important, regional allies must stop competing with each other for influence by provisioning different groups in an uncoordinated fashion and instead blend their efforts in a broader strategic plan with the Syrian fighters' commanders.

And we must understand two vital points going in:

—The moderate armed opposition's biggest enemy is not the Islamic State. It is the Assad regime which has killed far more Syrians than has the detestable Islamic State. And they won't stop fighting the Assad regime even as they advance against the Islamic State.
—Moreover, in the desperately hard-fought battle against the Assad regime, moderate forces have, and will, tactically coordinate with the al-Qaeda-linked Nusra Front on the ground. This is due to operational necessity, made more urgent by the shortage of supplies.

This coordination has nothing to do with ideological sympathy—indeed, groups such as the ones I mentioned have criticized the Nusra Front's politics and even refused to work with its leaders in towns recaptured from the regime.

Until the moderate elements are so strong that they don't need Nusra to pressure the regime successfully, the moderate elements will accept working militarily with Nusra.

As we think medium- and longer-term, a large moderate opposition force will be vital to holding ground seized back from the Islamic State. It will also be necessary to contain the Nusra Front one day. I do not see any other force that could do this short of a U.S.-led foreign force and even that would be extremely hard to sell politically in the region and in the broader international arena. I therefore welcome the administration's proposal to move to a Title 10 program.

However, just as in Iraq, the sustainable solution is to find a way to rally more Syrians against the Islamic State. The Assad regime's brutality has helped the Islamic State's rapid growth in Syria. Working with the Assad regime would be a golden gift to help the Islamic State's recruiting in Syria and beyond. And there aren't Assad forces to spare for central and eastern Syria anyway.

Instead, as in Iraq, the endgame in Syria has to be a new government able to rally the armed opposition and the remaining regime forces together to fight the Islamic State.

And we should know from the Libya experience, and our Iraq experience, that negotiating the creation of that new government in Syria, not trying to topple it, is the only way to preserve what remains of the Syrian state.

Getting to negotiations will be very, very hard. Our Geneva efforts failed quickly. But 7 months later, the regime's forces have taken heavy casualties at the hands of the Free Syrian Army and the Islamic State. Assad's remaining forces are more stretched and tired. There are new signs of dissent among Assad's ranks.

Asad's supporters may be tired but they don't see a place to jump. They fear extermination at the hands of the Islamic State and the al-Qaeda-linked Nusra Front. I don't blame them.

The best way to give them a sense that there is a third way for a new government—one that is neither the current regime nor an Islamic extremist state—is for the moderate opposition to reach out to Assad's supporters and to put forward ideas about how together they could assemble a new government.

Asad won't like this, but that's not the point. The point is that others inside the regime's ranks should and could drag the top Syrian leadership back to negotiations.

Thus, as we ramp up help to the Syrian moderate armed opposition, we also should insist that the opposition redouble efforts to reach out to regime elements and pursue discussions about a deal for a new government. There are steps the moderate opposition could take right now to send the right signal—treating prisoners well and offering to exchange them would be an excellent start.

I do not think any of this will be fast or easy. I do think that both sides are tiring, and that could help get to the negotiations for a new government. The conclusion of a few local cease-fire deals here and there indicates that local commanders at least are willing to talk.

Lastly, I welcome the administration's decision which, when implemented with real resources and actions, will gain support of regional allies. In Iraq when I was there we worked without regional support with the exception of Kuwait. The administration is making a strong pitch for regional political and material backing. If we show determination, the regional states who have long wanted to see the Syrian crisis resolved will back us, even if some necessarily do it quietly.

Going forward, we have be determined and committed.The first step is for the Congress to approve the President's proposal to help Syrian moderate armed groups. And as we begin our efforts under Title X and back moderate fighters on the ground, we will need to be strategically patient and very tough with our allies and the moderate opposition when they stray outside the agreed lines of scrimmage. The Islamic State problem has grown over the course of 3 years. Putting it down again in Iraq and Syria likely will last years more. But based on what I saw in Iraq years ago, it is achievable.

The CHAIRMAN. Thank you. Mr. Connable.

STATEMENT OF BEN CONNABLE, SENIOR INTERNATIONAL POLICY ANALYST, RAND CORPORATION, WASHINGTON, DC

Mr. CONNABLE. Chairman Menendez, Ranking Member Corker, and distinguished committee members, thank you for allowing me testify before you today on this critical topic. Ambassador Ford, it is an honor.

I have been engaging with Sunni Iraqis since 2003 first as a Marine intelligence officer in Iraq, then as an attaché in Amman, Jordan, and most recently in support of my research on Sunni-Iraqi perceptions at RAND. My remarks are based on those relationships and on my research.

This afternoon, I will outline options the United States and its allies can take in order to help free northern and western Iraq from Islamic State dominance. The thrust of my proposition here is that the success or failure of any coalition effort to defeat Islamic State and ultimately to stabilize Iraq hinges not on tactical consideration or tribal engagement efforts, but on the more critical issue of Sunni-Iraqi reconciliation.

IS has been able to dominate millions of Sunni with only a few thousand fighters because they generate considerable fear, but also because the ongoing Sunni revolt against the Government of Iraq has given IS a perfect opportunity to latch onto the Sunni host in a part parasitic, part symbiotic relationship. IS serves the purposes of the Sunni polity by fighting against the government, and the Sunni provide IS with at least a temporary accommodation.

In late 2014, we now have a situation in Iraq that closely resembles that in late 2004. Sunni Iraqis are disenfranchised from their government. They fear Iranian influence, and they do not yet trust the coalition. But underlying all of this is the desire to turn out the extremists. Tolerance of IS in Iraq is temporary. The ways in which they may be ejected, however, matter a great deal.

The coalition counterterrorism approach, which we use together with coalition airstrikes, Iraqi operations, and Sunni militia support, will certainly reduce IS influence and power in Iraq. Yet the coalition plan to defeat and destroy IS faces a range of challenges. I will enumerate three of those for you now.

First, the recent tactical victories in northern Iraq came only with the help of local sectarian and ethnic militias. It is possible, but unlikely, that these groups will directly support Iraqi army advances further west into the almost wholly-Sunni province of Al Anbar. There are limits to Iraqi collaboration.

Second, the offensive capability of the Iraqi army is questionable at best. They may well be able to mount a successful campaign into Mosul and Al Anbar, but it is more likely that they will move slowly, haltingly, and that they will have an insufficient force to overcome many of the hardened urban objectives they will face.

And third, the Iraqi army is not structured, trained, or inclined to conduct the kind of thoughtful counterinsurgency campaign that appears necessary in the Sunni provinces. Instead, they are likely to conduct the kind of tactical campaign they executed in Al Anbar in the first half of 2014. This military-centric approach is unlikely to generate grassroots Sunni support for the government.

Sunni popular and militia support, though, are critical to the success of the coalition campaign. This kind of uprising or revolt against IS is central to the possible solution I am laying before you this afternoon. To achieve this, some hope to force a reprise of the 2006 to 2008 awakening movement by aggressively incentivizing Sunni with financing and military aid. Yet simply paying or otherwise incentivizing Sunni to fight at the local level absent national reconciliation is likely to perpetuate rather than reduce instability in Iraq. If not addressed, the ongoing Sunni revolt will continue even if IS is ejected, in this event the second awakening is likely to end in the same was as the first, with Sunni fighters turning against the government in a recurring cycle of violence.

President Obama and senior administration officials have correctly stressed that success against IS is dependent on Iraqi reconciliation and positive Iraqi leadership. I recommend two mutually supporting approaches, one solely Iraqi and one for the broader coalition to capitalize on this strategic assumption. Prime Minister al-Abadi has a window of opportunity now in the early stages of the campaign to make unequivocal moves towards genuine reconciliation. The coalition should encourage him to enact all grievance resolution measures within his authority in one fell swoop.

Following this top-level Iraqi action, all coalition activities should be predicated on reconciliation. This may mean taking some tactical risk, but these risks will be taken in the hope of achieving long-term stability rather than short-term tactical success. Stopping IS now is wise. Current anti-IS action should be applied aggressively to keep the organization on its heels. In the case of IS, military force is necessary.

Yet addressing root causes of any insurgency has also historically proven to be the best and most lasting way to defeat insurgent groups. Leveraging reconciliation and using military force to support reconciliation rather than using reconciliation to support military force seems to be the least costly and possibly the only way to defeat Islamic State in Iraq and to stabilize that country.

I look forward to your questions. Thank you.

[The prepared statement of Mr. Connable follows:]

PREPARED STATEMENT OF BEN CONNABLE

Chairman [1] Menendez, Ranking Member Corker, and distinguished committee members, thank you for allowing me to testify before you today on this critical topic.

This afternoon I will first discuss how the self-described Islamic State, or IS, was able to sweep through northwestern Iraq with such rapidity, and then I will outline options the U.S. and its coalition allies might take in order to attempt to free northern and western Iraq from IS dominance. The thrust of my proposition here is that the success or failure of any coalition effort to defeat IS—and ultimately to stabilize Iraq—hinges not on tactical considerations or tribal engagement efforts, but on the more critical issue of Sunni Iraqi reconciliation. I believe the new anti-IS coalition can succeed if it predicates all of its actions in Iraq on national reconciliation between Sunni and Shia Iraqis. If political reconciliation is not the core aspect of an anti-IS strategy then coalition efforts are likely to fail in the long run.

ISLAMIC STATE SWEEPS INTO NORTHERN IRAQ

There are many tactical, or perhaps localized reasons why IS and its temporary nationalist insurgent allies were able to achieve so much success in June and July. These include a patient yet aggressive infiltration of IS assets into northern Iraq through the spring, major gaps in Iraqi Security Force (ISF) capabilities in Nineweh province, and also a series of IS victories in Syria and western Iraq that generated operational momentum. The Iraqi Army units in the Mosul area had alienated local Iraqis and lost nearly all vestiges of popular support. These units may have also been stripped of some of their equipment and personnel to shore up units fighting in Anbar province. Morale in the northern Iraqi Army Forces was low, leadership was weak, and IS capitalized brilliantly on their own operational surprise. Other Iraqi Army units that might have responded to the IS invasion of Mosul were tied down in the west or were simply incapable of the kind of rapid planning and movement required for operational-level quick reaction. IS succeeded in part because of Iraqi Army weakness, but also in great part due to their own military competence and elan.

All of these military factors were important to the IS sweep into northern Iraq. However, they do not fully explain why IS has been so successful in dominating millions of Sunni with only a few thousand fighters. The mostly Sunni Iraqi provinces of Anbar, Salah al-Din, and Nineweh are known for rejecting outside influence and repelling invaders. But while most Sunni Iraqis reject IS methods and philosophy, only a few have turned against IS and tried to push them out of the Sunni provinces. The ongoing Sunni revolt against the Government of Iraq (GoI) has given IS a perfect opportunity to latch on to the Sunni host in a part parasitic, part symbiotic relationship. IS serves the purposes of the Sunni polity by fighting against the government, and the Sunni provide IS with at least a temporary accommodation.

UNDERLYING SUNNI ISSUES PRESENT OPPORTUNITIES TO EXTREMISTS AND TO THE COALITION

A similar phenomenon took place between 2003 and 2006, the period after the U.S.-led coalition invasion of Iraq. Millions of Sunni Iraqis suffered the growth and ultimately the dominance of AQI while quietly and fearfully rejecting the al-Qaeda methods and philosophy. They underwent years of murder and intimidation, beheadings, robbery, and rape because at least in part they viewed AQI as the lesser of three evils: the extremist group did not present as great an existential threat as either a Shia-led government or the foreign coalition. During this period many nationalist, or Ba'athist fighters reached temporary deals with AQI and even supported some of its military activities. AQI's power culminated in early 2006 after

---

[1] The opinions and conclusions expressed in this testimony are the author's alone and should not be interpreted as representing those of RAND or any of the sponsors of its research. This product is part of the RAND Corporation testimony series. RAND testimonies record testimony presented by RAND associates to federal, state, or local legislative committees; government-appointed commissions and panels; and private review and oversight bodies. The RAND Corporation is a nonprofit research organization providing objective analysis and effective solutions that address the challenges facing the public and private sectors around the world. RAND's publications do not necessarily reflect the opinions of its research clients and sponsors.

the destruction of the Golden Mosque in Samaara; they exploited the fear of Shia oppression and took on the role of "defenders of the faithful" to fight for the Sunni.

Yet in late 2006 the Sunni Iraqis turned against AQI. Despite their best efforts to play on Sunni fears and sectarian animosities, AQI had worn out its welcome. Most Sunni Iraqi did not want to be part of an AQI caliphate and were only willing to accept AQI presence as long as the balance of fear kept them in check. The Awakening movement was the outward expression of the Sunni's turn against AQI. They accepted the promises of support and protection made by both the coalition and the government of Prime Minister al-Maliki. Many members of AQI turned against the group itself, other insurgents rose up to fight AQI emirs, and in very short order AQI was defeated. While coalition and Iraqi Army military power helped turn the tide, the key to success in 2006 and 2007 was the shift in popular Sunni sentiment against extremism and against outsider domination.

Unfortunately, Prime Minister al-Maliki abused the trust of the Sunni and undertook an active campaign to disenfranchise them. Between 2006 and 2013, the Sunni again lost faith in what they saw as an Iranian-influenced government. They again grudgingly allowed a foreign-led Sunni extremist group to enter and dominate their provinces, partly out of fear of IS and greatly out of fear of the Iraqi Security Forces (ISF). In late 2014 we now have a situation that closely resembles late 2004: Sunni Iraqis are disenfranchised from their government, they fear Iranian influence, and they do not yet trust the coalition. But underlying all of this is a desire to turn out the extremists. For now the members of IS float on the surface of the Sunni Iraqi polity; but they will never be integral nor will the Sunni Iraqis accept the IS caliphate. Tolerance of IS in Iraq is temporary. The ways in which they might be ejected, however, matter a great deal.

A MILITARY CENTRIC ANTI-IS EFFORT FACES FORMIDABLE CHALLENGES

In his 10 September speech, President Obama described a primarily military-focused effort designed to eject IS from Iraq and ultimately destroy them across the globe. This counterterrorism approach, which weaves together coalition airstrikes, Iraqi Army operations, and Sunni militia support, will certainly reduce IS influence and power in Iraq. Within months we can expect that IS armor, large artillery pieces, technical gun trucks, and overt fixed military positions will be reduced or eliminated inside of Iraq; they will no longer have the ability to conduct large-scale offensives of the kind we saw in Mosul and Tikrit. It does not necessarily follow, however, that IS will be weakened to the point of defeat. While many pundits and analysts have focused on IS technical and financial assets, their fighting power derives primarily from their overall morale and their aggressive, motivated small infantry units. Some of these can be destroyed from the air, but most can and probably will position themselves close to the civilian population in an effort to survive and increase chances of civilian casualties from airstrikes. As a result, airstrikes are insufficient to defeat or destroy IS.

The coalition plan also calls for increased support to the Iraqi Army, which will then help to drive IS out of Iraq. Equipment and trainers are already being prepared and deployed, and intelligence and air control support have already played critical roles in places like the Mosul Dam. All of these technical efforts will help Army units get back on their feet, and they will stiffen the resolve of some units that may be faltering. Consistent, overt U.S. military support can strengthen an allied partner in ways that cannot be measured and should not be underestimated. However, there are several reasons why the Iraqi Army will be challenged to achieve immediate or even long-term success against IS. I propose three of what I think are the most important reasons for doubt.

First, the recent tactical victories in northern Iraq came only with the help of combined Kurdish and Shia militia support. Iraqi Army units fought alongside Kurdistan Workers' Party (PKK) units, Peshmerga units, and some sectarian Shia fighters. It is possible but unlikely that Kurdish forces will directly support Iraqi Army advances into the mostly Sunni city of Mosul. It is even less likely they will support offensive thrusts further west into the almost wholly Sunni province of Anbar. They are most interested in protecting the Kurdish north. Similarly, Shia fighters are most interested in protecting their sectarian cantonments in Diyala and other mixed provinces. While some Shia militia may accompany Iraqi Army units west, their presence will only serve to reinforce the increasingly widespread—if perhaps exaggerated—belief amongst Sunni that the Iraqi Army is a Shia-dominated, Iranian-directed force bent on eliminating Sunni Arabs. There are limits to Iraqi collaboration.

Second, the offensive capability of the Iraqi Army is questionable at best. They may well be able to mount a successful campaign into Mosul and Anbar, but it is more likely that they will move slowly, haltingly, and that they will have insufficient force to overcome hardened urban objectives. They remain, as some experts have noted, logistically challenged; this problem will require years of remediation. Iraqi special operations forces that have carried out the most aggressive and successful actions against Sunni insurgents are exhausted from nearly a year of constant combat, and they are too few in number to generate the kind of combat power necessary to seize a large urban area like Mosul, Fallujah, or Ramadi.

And third, the Iraqi Army is not structured, trained, or inclined to conduct the kind of thoughtful counterinsurgency campaign that appears necessary in the Sunni provinces. Instead they are likely to conduct the kind of counterguerrilla campaign they executed in Anbar in the first half of 2014. Counterinsurgency campaigns are designed to win support of the population by building government legitimacy and applying force in careful measure. Counterguerrilla campaigns are designed to kill guerrillas, or in this case IS. In early 2014 Iraqi Army units conducted Vietnam War era ''sweep and clear'' missions across Anbar province with very little success. When they moved against the insurgent stronghold in Fallujah they used excessive force and still failed to retake the city. Surely they will be more successful at killing IS fighters with coalition air support and intelligence, but they will probably be no more successful at winning popular support than they were earlier this year.

There are also aspects of IS that will affect the likelihood of military success. I stated previously that they are militarily competent and resilient. They may collapse in the face of airstrikes and ground offensives, but it seems more likely that they will adapt their tactics and dig into dense urban areas. They will also probably accelerate their use of terror attacks against both military and civilian targets in order to weaken political support for the coalition and to degrade Iraqi Army morale.

But while IS has many strengths it also has weaknesses. As pressure mounts against the group, and as young and unbalanced IS fighters are forced to manage hundreds of thousands of Sunni civilians, the likelihood that IS will alienate the Sunni Iraqis increases. And while IS may have a robust force of tens of thousands of fighters across Iraq and Syria, some IS fighters were either forcibly conscripted or have stronger loyalties to Iraqi nationalist insurgent groups like the Jaysh al-Rijal al-Tariqeh al-Naqshibandieh, or JRTN. These conscripts and nationalist fighters can be peeled away from IS with the right pressure and incentives. This will make the job of the Iraqi Army somewhat easier.

WHAT ABOUT THE TRIBES? CONSIDERING A SECOND AWAKENING MOVEMENT

There are challenges to an Iraqi Army offensive, even if it is supported by coalition airstrikes and intelligence. But there are three proposed legs to the anti-IS military plan: airstrikes, Iraqi Army operations, and Sunni popular support. Ostensibly the Iraqi Government and the coalition will try to rally Sunni support to turn against IS and, at the very least, defend their local areas to create space for the Iraqi Army to maneuver. Some hope to see a reprise of the 2006–08 Awakening Movement. A mass Sunni uprising against IS would probably shift the balance of power in favor of the government and might rapidly push IS back across the international border to Syria. Indeed, this uprising, or revolt against IS is central to the possible solution I am laying before you this afternoon. However, it is important to eliminate misconceptions about the first Awakening movement before trying to encourage a second.

Conditions in 2006 and early 2007 were perfect for an Awakening. AQI had alienated the population, the U.S. had demonstrated its commitment to the Iraqis by announcing a surge of troops, and the Iraqi Government pledged millions of dollars in reconstruction support to Sunni areas stricken by years of heavy combat. Finely tuned special operations targeting raids kept the insurgents on their heels while U.S. infantry and armored forces created safe zones for civilians and for burgeoning yet vulnerable Sons of Iraq militias. Prime Minister al-Maliki offered reconciliation to the Sunni and seemed to prove his nonsectarian bona fides by moving against Shia militias. And probably millions of dollars changed hands through local reconstruction deals and direct payments to fund and motivate Sunni militia leadership.

What did not happen is just as important as what did happen. While Sattar Albu Risha did lead the Awakening council and was a charismatic figure, he was not a unifying figure for all Sunni nor did he generate the Awakening. At no point did U.S. interlocutors find ''the right person'' to talk with, thereby energizing a Sunni revolt against AQI. Instead, Albu Risha was a convenient public face for a broad grassroots shift in popular sentiment. And while the U.S. troop surge played an important moral and physical role in defeating AQI, the troop surge was not the critical component in the Awakening. While it would have been far more difficult, and would have taken longer, it is possible that the Awakening might have succeeded against AQI even with less U.S. or coalition support. Iraqi Sunni are competent and sometimes aggressive fighters. They nearly ejected the coalition from Iraq, and perhaps ultimately they could have ejected AQI from Sunni-dominated areas.

Conditions today are different in several critical ways. IS has alienated many Sunni, but it still has some support in various Sunni areas. There are some strong local Sunni leaders and even potential national leaders, but the Sunni political class is badly fragmented. Even tribal leaders have very limited influential power over their own tribal members, and many tribes are if anything more divided than they were in 2006. There are no U.S. ground troops to create "oil spots" of stability for fledgling militia forces, and ostensibly none of the supremely capable U.S. special operations direct action forces will help pick apart IS leadership in the dense urban or maze-like rural swathes of Anbar. Most importantly, though, is the absence of proof—so far—that the new Prime Minister of Iraq, Haider al-Abadi, is serious about reconciliation.

Finding "the right person" to talk to amongst Iraq's Sunnis and handing over bags of cash to stand up militias or encourage Sunni to join a new national guard may lead to real short-term tactical success in some Sunni areas of Iraq. There may be visible signs of Sunni resistance against IS as tribal leaders come to the fore and, cash in hand, pledge to work alongside the Iraqi Army. It is possible that over time, with coalition airpower, the Iraqi Army and Sunni militiamen may be able to push IS out of Iraq without national reconciliation of any kind.

Ultimately, though, this quick tactical approach is likely to perpetuate rather than reduce instability in Iraq. While the world focuses on IS, it is important to remember that IS floats above the Sunni population and does not represent enduring Sunni grievances or narratives. There is an ongoing Sunni revolt against the Iraqi Government that, if not addressed, will continue even if IS is ejected.

In this event the second Awakening is likely to end in the same way as the first: with armed, angry Sunni fighters turning against the government in a recurring cycle of violence.

I propose there is a way to encourage the Sunni to turn against IS in a way that will be more tactically effective, more cost effective, and ultimately more enduring than inducing quick and temporary allegiances with cash and military aid. I also propose that this approach will obviate the weaknesses inherent in a primarily military or counterterror approach to the IS problem.

RECONCILIATION IS THE BEST AND LEAST COSTLY OPTION FOR SUCCESS

The Iraqi state that existed in early 2014 now exists only in the Iraqi Constitution. There is a de facto split of Iraq along ethnosectarian lines: Sunni, Shia, and Kurd. It may or may not be possible to bring the Kurds fully back into the Iraqi state. Chances for successful Sunni-Shia reconciliation are probably quite low. However, my interactions with Sunni Iraqis since 2003, and my targeted research on Sunni Iraqi perceptions over the past year indicate that all strata of the Sunni Iraqi population wish to remain within the state.

They tend to view their revolt against the government as an anti-Iranian rather than an anti-Shia movement. Most are nationalists who believe they should play a prominent role in the central state. Further, the natural resources in the Sunni provinces are inconsequential in comparison to Kurdish and Shia resources, and Sunni do not believe decentralization will result in equitable sharing. While they want more local power, they do not want to be permanently marginalized and disenfranchised from the state. It is therefore possible to leverage Sunni nationalism to foster lasting reconciliation.

One approach to Sunni reconciliation would be through negotiation. This might require finding a charismatic Sunni leader who represents a large majority, or at least large plurality, of the Sunni population. His influence would have to be sufficient to encourage tens of thousands of Sunni to turn against IS. As of late-2014, though, this leader has not emerged and the Sunni do not seem disposed to follow a single political figure. Another approach would be dispersed engagement, with coalition and Iraqi leaders fanning out across Iraq to drum up local support. I argue this approach will lead to tactical success but strategic failure. Instead, I propose that only intensive, one-sided national reconciliation efforts aimed at the broad Sunni population will lead to lasting success.

Earlier this month Prime Minister al-Abadi enumerated a list of grievance resolution measures he intended to take in order to win Sunni support. These include general amnesty for innocent Sunni caught up in the counterguerrilla campaign, a depoliticized justice system, amendments to antiterror laws, reconstruction of damaged Sunni areas, the formation of a National Guard, and increased regional authorities. Sunni leaders have listed other grievances and want the immediate release of all female prisoners and Sunni politicians, restoration of full retirement pay for former regime officers, and other measures to reduce the impact of de-Ba'athification laws that have been used to target Sunni leadership. Some of these actions will require political ratification, but others will not.

President Obama and senior administration officials have correctly stressed that success against IS is dependent on Iraqi reconciliation and on positive Iraqi leadership. Prime Minister al-Abadi has a window of opportunity now, in the early stages of the campaign, to make unequivocal moves toward genuine reconciliation. The coalition should encourage him to enact all grievance resolution measures within his authority in one fell swoop. This action, which should include prisoner releases and the real-time transfer of money for reconstruction and retirement pay, would demonstrate that he is taking a different path than his predecessor. At this point in the year-long Sunni revolt, only real and dramatic action on the above-named fronts will be sufficient to convince the Sunni that the more tangible things—cash payments, equipment—are part of a broader strategy to reunite the state.

Following this top-level Iraqi action, all coalition activities should be predicated on reconciliation. Every engagement should hinge on some kind of local or regional reconciliation measure, and every tactical military action should be planned to preserve and improve relationships between the Sunni and the state. This may mean taking some tactical risk, including strictly limiting damage to Sunni urban areas and curtailing aerial targeting. Advisors will find themselves in difficult positions as they attempt to rein in Iraqi Army air and artillery support. This approach will certainly preclude the use of Shia and Kurdish militias in support of Iraqi Army combat actions in Sunni areas. Reconciliation first and foremost, in conjunction with coalition support, and Iraqi military and government efforts must be woven together into a holistic strategy with a definitive envisioned end-state.

There are many hurdles to successful reconciliation. Divisions in the Sunni polity will continue to undermine Sunni cohesion and may hinder efforts to develop militia support. Prime Minister al-Abadi may not be willing or able to make the kind of dramatic measures necessary to gain Sunni trust. And IS and some of its allies will probably make every effort to foster discord between Sunni and Shia in order to maintain Sunni support. They already conduct terror attacks that seem designed to deepen the divide between Sunni and Shia Iraqis. However, there are also some positive underlying factors. While there are divisions between Sunni and Shia Iraqis, there are also strong inter- and intra-tribal bonds between the two sectarian groups. Sunni leaders I have spoken with in the last year repeatedly emphasized their belief that Sunni and Shia Iraqis are first and foremost Iraqis.

CONCLUSION

As I stated earlier, chances of genuine and lasting reconciliation in Iraq are admittedly low. However, reconciliation also offers the best and perhaps only chance to reconstitute the admittedly limited successes of Operation Iraqi Freedom and Operation New Dawn. Absent reconciliation we can expect lasting instability in Iraq. We may physically defeat IS, but the ideas that cause young Iraqi men to support groups like IS and al-Qaeda will live on. The group name will change—there were over 100 identified insurgent groups in Iraq during the 2003–11 war—but the violence will continue to destabilize the region, give space for international terror groups, and deprive millions of Iraqis of even a modicum of normal life.

Stopping IS now is wise; current anti-IS actions should be applied aggressively to keep the group on its heels. In the case of IS, military force is necessary. Yet addressing root causes of any insurgency is also historically proven to be the best and most lasting way to defeat insurgent groups. Leveraging reconciliation—and using military force to support reconciliation rather than using reconciliation to support military force—seems to be the least costly and possibly the only way to defeat IS in Iraq and stabilize that country.

The CHAIRMAN. Well, thank you both for your testimony. Ambassador Ford, let me start with you. One of the main arguments that the administration has presented in addressing members of Congress' concerns about the vetting for the fighters that we seek to train and equip—the so-called moderate vetted Syrian rebels—is we know them. We know them. And I can tell you that as this issue has come forward that I am constantly called by colleagues for which this is one of their central questions—not their only question, but it is one of their central questions, particularly as this vote comes up.

So my questions to you are: do we really know these fighters would receive U.S. training and equipping if Congress provides the authority? And are there enough willing, capable fighters that would pass U.S. vetting standards, do you believe?

Ambassador FORD. The answer to the second question is a simple, yes, there will be enough. Actually the problem has always been, Senator Menendez, that there have been more willing fighters in the Free Syrian Army than they have material guns, ammunition, et cetera.

So a different question is, do we know them? Two things I would say. First, we do not know all 1,500 groups because some of the groups are just two or three guys and, you know, they have a video camera, and, wow, you are, you know, a group of freedom fighters. There is actually a pretty small number of serious groups, and when I say ''serious,'' I mean that have a thousand, two, five, 7,000. That number of groups is actually pretty small. It would not pass more than about 15 to 20. Funny how that is never mentioned in the press.

Those groups, we do not work with all of them. Some of them are beyond the pale politically in terms of not being moderate the way I mentioned, like Ahrar ash-Sham, which has sectarian tendencies and might well try to impose a state. And that is a big group. So I have met Ahrar ash-Sham, but we do not in any way provide assistance to them.

But the other groups and the ones that, for example, the State Department was providing nonlethal assistance to, yes, we know them. Not a secret that I have met them on occasion in places like Turkey, and I went over the border and met them in Syria about 14 months ago. We know them, and we have talked politics with them. We have talked about the Nusra Front with them. Those, I think, we know, and we have had more experience just in the last 7, 8, 9, 10 months with them as well. So I think the groups that we need to help that will have an impact on the ground, we know them.

The CHAIRMAN. Okay. So we know them, and you believe that a sufficient number of capable fighters would pass U.S. vetting standards.

Ambassador FORD. Yes, I feel very strongly about that.

The CHAIRMAN. All right. Well, that is very important to know. Now, in an article in Sunday's New York Times, there was a report that said, ''Mr. Assad and his closest advisors have looked at the American decision to undertake anti-ISIL military strikes in Syria as representing a victory for their longstanding strategy, which is obliterating any moderate opposition to its rule, and persuading the world that it faces a stark choice between him and the Islamist militants who threaten the West.''

How do we respond to those who raise that concern? How do we prevent Assad and his Iranian- and Russian-backed forces from seizing back territory from ISIL after military strikes, further squeezing the moderate vetted Syrian rebels?

Ambassador FORD. Two comments on that very quickly, Senator. First, Assad does not have enough forces. He has been seriously depleted. That is why he could not hold the air base in Tabqa, for example, where they actually flew some of their senior officers out and then left hundreds of their soldiers to be murdered by the Islamic State of Iraq and Levant. And they could not hold other parts of eastern Syria, for example.

He does not have the troops to put back in. His forces are very stretched. He was depending a lot on Hezbollah and Iraqi Shia militia. The Iraqi Shia militiaq has flown home to deal with ISIL inside Iraq.

So I would not worry so much, especially in north and eastern Syria about Assad benefiting very much. The moderate armed opposition will benefit greatly more, especially as they try to secure their supply lines. It is interesting to me that ISIL is trying to cut their supply lines coming down from Turkey. So they need to—they need help to secure those lines.

One other comment about Bashir al-Assad. I think his strategy all along has been to sort of destroy the political opposition—the moderate political opposition and the armed fighters attached to it. If we do not go forward on this proposal to help the moderate armed opposition, I think he will say indeed my strategy is working, the Americans will come around and eventually deal with me. And that will actually make it even harder to get a resolution to the Syrian crisis.

The CHAIRMAN. Which is, in part, why we had an authorization in the committee a year ago, which supported your view. Part of what I want to do here is try to get some of the concerns of my colleagues responded to by virtue of your expertise.

Secondly—thirdly, the authorization language submitted by the administration in order to stand up, train, and equip the effort for the Syrian moderate opposition articulates three purposes: one, defending the Syrian people from attacks by ISIL and the Syrian regime, facilitating the provisions of essential services and stabilizing territory controlled by the opposition; two, protecting the United States, its friends and allies, and the Syrian people from the threats posed by terrorists in Syria; and, three, promoting the conditions of a negotiated settlement to end the conflict in Syria. Do you agree that those should be the stated purposes? Would you change or add anything to them?

Ambassador FORD. Sorry. I had not seen the language. Yes. These seem reasonable to me, but I would just caution that getting to negotiations is going to be a very long and hard process. I would not want to pretend that we could get there quickly. Geneva was a bad failure, and until the regime feels more pressure—it is already under pressure. What is interesting is in Assad's own community now, there are demonstrations against him. There is a whole campaign called Sarkhet al-Watan—''Scream of the na- tion''—just criticizing Assad for keeping his throne, they call it, and sending young Alawis to their graves. So there is—there are cracks which we did not see before. But I do not think this is going to be fast, Senator.

So the first goal of containing and starting to roll back ISIL and defending the Syrian people, and also as well protecting us, those are in the short term things we have to work on right way. Negotiations are going to come later.

The CHAIRMAN. Right. And do you think—I think—oh, Senator McCain is back, so he is probably going to ask this question on his own, but I think it is an important one. Do you envision the moderate vetted Syrian rebels understanding that if we are training and equipping them with our focus being ISIL that they will look toward that fight even as their main goal is to displace Assad?

Ambassador FORD. Absolutely they will for two reasons. One, the Islamists, or ISIL, is actually threatening their supply lines right now, and has butchered hundreds of members of the moderate Syrian opposition, and I mean butchered. Cut their throats, video, the whole nine yards. So there is no—there is a lot of bad blood between them. That is the first reason.

The second reason is, in places where ISIL was in authority, especially in northwestern Syria in the Idlib province, there was a popular reaction against them. And that public popular support helped the moderate armed opposition actually eject ISIL fighters out of that province. And also the same thing happened in Aleppo to the west of the city.

There was also an uprising, Senator, a very big uprising against ISIL. In Deir ez-Zor province, an entire tribe, called Shaitat tribe, rose up against them, but they did not—they did not get any help. And that is not a criticism of us per se, but they just—they lost a military battle, and ISIL killed—I have seen estimates of as many as a thousand of the tribesmen afterwards in retaliation. So there will be constant problems and fighting between the moderate armed opposition and ISIL. I do not see any way that that is going to end.

Syrians just in general are Mediterranean people, and they do not go for this kind of very heavy duty, conservative Salafi type state. They are just not that kind of fundamentalist religiously.

The CHAIRMAN. Well, these insights are very important. Mr. Connable, I do have questions for you, but my time has run out. In deference to my colleagues, I will come back to you at the end.

Senator Corker.

Senator CORKER. Thank you, Mr. Chairman, and, again, thank you for this hearing today. Thank you both for your testimony. Ambassador Ford, I think we have all experienced being in—or most of us—refugee camps looking into the eyes of Syrians who had counted on us to do a lot of things that we said we were going to do and did not do. And their brothers, and cousins, and uncles were butchered, and we never supported them like we said we would.

You actually encouraged them out doing your patriotic duty. We encouraged them out. And, in fact, we did not follow up with much that they thought was coming, and when we did, it was delayed. And I want to thank you for your service also and your leadership in Syria. And I think all of us on this panel probably wish to do so.

My question to you is, what is the mentality now of the Syrian opposition having seen, you know, promised support, it not being what was envisioned? What is their mentality, their attitude, toward the United States right now relative to helping them, if you will, against Assad?

Ambassador FORD. Senator Corker, thank you. First, just a comment to be clear on the record, we did not encourage, and I certainly as Ambassador did not encourage Syrians to protest. But I did defend their right to protest peacefully. And, in fact, when I was in the country I said, do not resort to violence because it will cause problems even for us if you do that. That is ancient history. But just to be clear what we did, we did not encourage them out, but we absolutely stood for their right to protest peacefully in accord with rights under the U.N. Charter for Human Rights.

What is the mentality of the Syrian opposition now toward us? I think you and I both know that there is a lot of bitterness. Two hundred, maybe more—200,000 maybe more have died. I think there is very great anger that the United States did not intervene militarily to stop that. There is a belief that we could have stopped it. I am not sure that belief is accurate, but in any case it is widely held. And so, we have a credibility problem, and we have a credibility problem, Senator Corker, with some of these groups even.

You do not regain credibility overnight. It is based on new shared experiences. And so, were we to go forward with the administration's proposal, and I certainly hope we do, I think with the passage of time, credibility and confidence can be restored. But I think it will be bumpy at the start.

Senator CORKER. One of the things that people—thank you for that. One of the things—one of the things that people have said, and by the way, I strongly supported, as most people did here, arming, especially back in May, but even before, a year and a half ago. And I think we might be in a different situation, and I would say we would be in a different situation today if we had taken action at a more—at a better time. I still support what is getting ready to happen, although I have a lot of questions relative to the moderate opposition being trained and armed.

Some people have said who have been close to this issue that there are not enough—I know you answered a question specifically to Menendez, but there are not enough, and it is very difficult and expensive to train these people, that 5,000 troops over the next year, short-term training in Saudi Arabia, getting more sophisticated weapons after they have proven themselves on the ground is something that is not going to be particularly effective. Could you respond to that?

Ambassador FORD. Syria is a big country, Senator, and 5,000 is not a lot for a country that size. The Syrian armed opposition, however, is a lot bigger than 5,000. I think the latest numbers I have seen for the non-Nusra, non-ISIL groups is still in the range of 80 to 100,000. I think most people now are saying it is more on the lower end of that, so say 80,000. Some say higher. The Islamic State—you probably saw the same things in the press I did. They have somewhere 20 to 30,000, of which some are in Iraq and some are in Syria.

So it is not as if the 5,000 would be the only ones on the field. I think there will be a lot of others on the field. And although we are not helping some of the harder line Islamist groups, like Ahrar ash-Sham, Ahrar ash-Sham is also fighting ISIL right now, and ISIL killed a number of Ahrar ash-Sham prisoners. And so we are not in that exact fight, and the groups that we have helped are not in that fight. But there are other people also fighting the Islamic State. So I do not look at it as only 5,000.

Senator CORKER. Knowing what you know about the way things are on the ground, is what is being laid out something that will evolve into an effective ground strategy, or are there additional components that you knowing the country the way you do are necessary—if we really want to destroy and defeat ISIL are necessary to make that happen?

Ambassador FORD. I would think we are going to get into a longer-term relationship with some of these groups that I mentioned. It needs to be really carefully coordinated with other countries in the region that have been funneling in help. And it has got to be centralized in a way, Senator. There is too much stuff going to too many disparate groups, and it actually has made the job of the armed opposition much more difficult. So we are going to have to be pretty tough with some of our regional allies. That is on the diplomatic political side.

On the ground, Senator, as ISIL is pushed out of places, it will be really important to try to get help into the civil administrations. The Syrian Government will not go into those places. And, again, these are in a sense the political side of the opposition linked to the moderate armed opposition. And so, the State Department has worked in some places with these people, and I think there is going to have to be a dedication of resources and program money to backfill as ISIL is pushed out of places so that the lights stay on some hours a day, so that there is clean water some hours of the day, maybe so schools can reopen in some places, that kind of thing.

Senator CORKER. Just one more question. I know time is short. We put a lot of stock in Idris, and many of us got to know him, and yet we did not support him. We left him hanging. Trucks that were supposed to be delivered to him were delivered months late. The things—I mean, it was almost like a—I do not even want to use the word because it is just a negative connotation toward the activities that we undertook. Has there been a command and control established for the moderate opposition that is workable after we, in essence, again, undermined by not really doing the things we said we would do, not that Idris was General Patton. But do we have someone there, an organization there, that has the ability to deal with command and control?

Ambassador FORD. I think this is a question that you will want to be asking as you go forward. You are right, Idris was never empowered not only by us, Senator, but by other regional states that were funneling assistance in. And so, he was always in a very difficult position. And I think going forward, if we want the moderate armed opposition to be successful, we are going to have to figure out a way to get a more centralized command structure. And aid goes through that structure, and all countries must support that structure and not help friendly group over here or friendly group over there.

The CHAIRMAN. Senator Rubio.

Senator RUBIO. Thank you. Thank you both for being here, and thank you, Ambassador. A couple of points that I wanted to—first, I do not want to go back in time simply for purposes of pointing fingers or saying who was wrong and who was right, but I think it is important to learn lessons from this.

It was my impression early in this conflict that when this arose, and by the way, it is important to remind everyone that this was not a U.S.-instigated thing. These were Syrians who wanted to get rid of Assad. And in the initial stages, the rebellion were Syrians, but the lack of—the decision not to go in and empower them early created a vacuum that attracted foreign fighters from all over the world to kind of pour in and take advantage of that situation.

In your opinion, had we been more forceful early on—if we could go back two and half years in time knowing what we know especially and had empowered those groups early on to be more capable, do you think that it is possible that you would—that that space that was left there for ISIL may never have existed? In essence, having a more forceful group on the ground, you know, the Syrian military defectors early on would have closed off the opening for some of these more radical foreign fighters to be able to come in and take advantage of the chaos on the ground?

Ambassador FORD. Senator, I do think that. I have said that publicly before. And in particular, three things: cash, ammunition, and food. And had more of the moderate groups I am talking about that are not seeking to impose an Islamic state by force, had they had these things—cash, ammo, food—in greater supplies in, say, second half of 2012, it would have been very hard for Nusra to gain recruits. I heard that repeatedly from members of the Syrian opposition, including from the Free Syrian Army, that they could not pay salaries. The other guys could.

I would say, well, I mean, you are a liberation movement; why do you need salaries? And they would say, you have got to understand, the fighters have families. They have got kids. They have got parents they have to take care of. So, yes, if there had been more back then, I think the problem today would be smaller, but I am encouraged at least that now I think there is an understanding of that. And if this program goes forward, I think that will actually help reduce the recruiting of ISIL and Nusra.

Senator RUBIO. Now, the second question I wanted to ask, and it touches upon a theme that Senator McCain has also explored is, so these groups that are on the ground that we want to work with now, as you said in your testimony, the biggest threat that they face, the people who are targeting them right now the most, although they will fight ISIL. But the group that is doing the most damage to them militarily is Assad.

It seems from here to appear to be that Assad is undertaking a very deliberate strategy of trying to wipe out what we could call moderate forces so that the world is left with a very simple choice: if you want to defeat ISIL in Syria, you have to align yourself with Assad. He is the only alternative to them, if he can wipe these more moderate groups out.

And then, in fact, it seems like over the last few hours, days, and weeks, he has ramped up the effort to wipe them out in pursuance of that strategy. Do you agree that is the calculation he has made? And, if so, how could any effort to equip and empower and capacitate these groups, how could any effort to do that be successful if we do not protect them from the assault that is being undertaken against them?

As I asked the Secretary when he was here, I guess, 2 hours ago now, when I asked him questions, there may not be anyone left for us to arm or train if Assad is continued to be given free rein to target them and try to eviscerate them.

Ambassador FORD. I do think that is Assad's strategy, and I think it is very evident. Just kind of looking at what he is doing day by day, it is clear. I do think the moderate armed opposition has some staying power, and if the administration's proposals are adopted and go forward, I think that will help bolster them, and they will be in the field for the long term.

But absolutely they are going to fight Bashir al-Assad. I think the idea that they would somehow turn away from that fight, the original fight, and focus solely on ISIL is simply not realistic.

Senator RUBIO. Well, they cannot ignore the fact they are being attacked.

Ambassador FORD. Right, precisely. And in the end, I talked about the bad blood between ISIL and the armed moderate opposition, but there is plenty of bad blood between them and the Assad regime, too, not to mention the airstrikes you are talking about.

I do take heart, Senator Rubio, that the armed moderate opposition, I think they have gotten more supplies, though. I am not sure where from. But they have been making some gains on the ground, and, in particular, against the Syrian regime, and in particular, up in the area between Damascus and Aleppo, Hama and Homs up there. There is a lot of heavy fighting, and also along the Lebanese border in a place called Qalamoun where the moderate armed opposition suffered a big defeat in May and June 2013. They have actually retaken a lot of those places. And I think part of it is Hezbollah had to re-deploy to other places, and this just goes back to the manpower shortage of the regime itself.

So as we go to the American people and we make the argument we need to do this, and I am in favor of doing this. I have actually called for this for quite a while, and I was part of those on this committee that voted to do that a while back. The American people best understand when they—either a face or a name that they know. Right now it is just kind of a generic term, ``moderate rebels,'' but we do not know who they are. And in the absence of being able to point to who they are, it leaves it open to all sorts of misinformation that I have seen in the press, including from members of Congress who have made claims that, quite frankly, are not only inaccurate, but outrageous with regards to who some of these groups are and who we would be working with.

Could you help navigate a couple of the organizations? I mean, I know there are some groups out there that we have heard. The Steadfastness Movement is one. I do not know if you are familiar with them. Harakat Hazm, but other groups like this. I mean, I do not know if that is the right example, but who exactly are some of these groups that you think fit the bill of what we would look to work with?

Ambassador FORD. Yes. So let me—I will just very quickly name a few, and they are in my written testimony, and I am happy to provide members of your staffs more information later. Harakat Hazm, the Hazzm Movement, which operate mainly in northern Syria, but also has fighters in the south. They are one of the groups. They actually are kind of more or less fighting the Nusra front right now, as well as the Islamic State and the regime. And so, they are in it up to their eyeballs.

There are two units of the moderate opposition that are mainly officered by recently defected Syrian army officers. One is called the 101st Division, although I do not think it has anywhere near a division's worth of men. I think it is in the range of 3,000 to 4,000. The 101st—it is kind of ironic—too bad Dave is not here. And then the 13th Division as well, again, led primarily by recently defected army officers.

You might remember, Senator Rubio, there was a Syrian air force pilot who flew his plane to Jordan a couple of years ago. That pilot is the commander of the 13th Division now. But it is not a division in terms of, like, 14, 15,000. There are a couple of thousand.

The CHAIRMAN. Senator Johnson.

Senator JOHNSON. Thank you, Mr. Chairman. Ambassador Ford, you mentioned a word that really—I really want to be the crux of my questioning, is "credibility." I want to explore the credibility of our commitment and the credibility of our strategy.

So, first of all, in my questioning of Secretary Kerry, I quoted the President when he said that "Our safety, our security depends on our willingness to do whatever it takes to defend this Nation." And, of course, by taking off—a number of options off the table, I certainly am concerned about that, the credibility of our commitment.

What is your view in terms of our potential coalition partners? I mean, they are listening to this as well. Do they feel there is any credibility to our commitment to the defeat of ISIS?

Ambassador FORD. I think the meeting in Riyadh was really interesting—I am sorry—in Jeddah. I was really struck that the Saudis brought the Iraqi Foreign Minister there, and that was something when I was working in Iraq for 5 years under—during the war with all of our ambassadors there, we could never get the Saudis to do that. Never could get the Saudis to do that. So I think that is a change, and it is significant. It is symbolic, but it is a start.

I think ultimately, Senator Johnson, our credibility by countries in that region—Saudi, Emirates, Qatar, Turkey—will be judged by what we do ourselves in the next few weeks and months. If the proposal to help the Syrian armed opposition does not move forward out of Washington this week and then gets bogged down, I think our credibility will suffer not only with the Syrian opposition, but it will suffer with countries in the region.

Senator JOHNSON. So let me quickly ask, is it true that the Saudis are willing to base as well as pay for that training effort?

Ambassador FORD. I have not received any classified briefings since I left government, Senator Johnson, but it seems everything I am seeing in both Arabic language media as well as English language media says it is the case.

Senator JOHNSON. I mean, if that is the case, then let us face it, the moderate-vetted Syrian rebels will be armed and trained. So would it make sense—that being the case, would it not be better for the United States to be involved in that training, especially if we do not have to pay for it?

Ambassador FORD. Completely. Totally.

Senator JOHNSON. Okay. Again, I think that is the political argument for voting for that authorization.

Ambassador FORD. I am assuming—again, I have not received any classified briefings. You all will know more than I do, but I am assuming that there will be U.S. personnel working on this with Saudis and other coalition partners in Saudi Arabia.

Senator JOHNSON. Yes, I would just make that point because— I make that point. I understand our colleagues' concern about who are we really training, but they are going to be trained anyway. I would rather be involved in that process, probably reduce the chance that the wrong individuals will be trained by whoever.

Ambassador FORD. We will be much safer from ISIL in the future if we lead this effort rather than hand it off to someone else.

Senator JOHNSON. Mr. Connable, you have been sitting here. There you go. I do want to actually utilize you in the testimony here. I want to really talk about the credibility of the strategy. From my standpoint, there is really two major steps to the offense. I mean, first of all, it is to drive ISIS out of Iraq and secure Iraq again, and then, of course, we have got the whole mess in terms of Syria.

Let us go back in history. I think both you gentlemen were there in Iraq during the surge. We had Brett McGurk before us, and I was just trying to kind of put this thing in context using some numbers. We had about 68,000 Al Qaeda in Iraq at that point in time were the estimates, and we had 130,000—surged over 160,000 U.S. troops to defeat Al Qaeda in Iraq. Now we have got 31,000 ISIS. We have 1,500 noncombat troops on the ground. We have got an Iraqi Security Force. We have the Kurdish Peshmerga. How credible is it that we are going to be able to, first of all, just get ISIS out of Iraq with that force?

Mr. CONNABLE. I would start by saying I do not put a lot of credence in the numbers that we had either in the first Iraq war that we have now. I do not believe we have any degree of accuracy there, so assuming we are within some kind of order of magnitude there.

I do not think the key to this in 2006, 2007, and 2008 was necessarily the surge. The announcement of the surge helped strengthen our allies on the ground. Really I believe it was the Sunni population turning against Al Qaeda in Iraq that was the key to victory there. And I think that is going to be the key to victory now.

So whether there are 10,000 IS in Iraq or 30,000, I think over time that becomes less relevant when you look at how much territory they have to control. If that is hostile territory, they are going to have a real hard time doing that. Just bombing them and trying to drive them out with Iraqi army units, I think our chances are much lower.

Senator JOHNSON. So which gets you basically to your point that the key here is reconciliation between the Sunni and the Shia in Iraq. And I guess the question I wanted to ask either one of you or both of you—I am trying to think of the exact term you used— the grievance resolution measures. Is the Shia government threat enough to actually do what you think is necessary to pass those grievance resolution measures to bring the Sunnis back into the government?

Mr. CONNABLE. Frankly, I think the chances of reconciliation are low. I think it is the best strategy, and it is probably the one that is going to lead to long-term success. But Haider al-Abadi is in a very difficult position. He has got the Iranians there providing direct support. They have no enthusiasm for reconciliation with Iraqi-Sunni. He has got other fragmented elements of the Shia polity that he has to deal with. They just voted down a couple of his nominations for key posts in his cabinet. So I do not hold out a great deal of hope, but I do think that that is where we need to put all our emphasis.

Senator JOHNSON. So in other words—go ahead, Ambassador Ford.

Ambassador FORD. I totally agree with what Ben said, that the key to the success in Iraq back in the period 2007, 2008, 2009 was getting Sunni Arab support. The presence of our troops was vital, but the most important part, the key part, was to get the buy-in from the local populations.

Just one little thing on your question about are the Shia today, 2014, are they sobered. Ben is absolutely right. The nominees for Defense and Interior Minister are such sensitive positions in the cabinet that were just disapproved by the Iraqi Parliament yesterday. Not a good sign. However, I have also seen Prime Minister al-Abadi say they will not send the Iraqi Army deep into Sunni regions again, and that they are going to try to build a national guard. I have seen him say that.

So I think now what they are arguing about in Iraq, if I understand it is, who do they trust enough from among the Shia and the Sunni to do that mission. So the proof will be in the pudding. Having spent 5 years in Iraq, I have learned to trust nothing at first look. But I at least was encouraged that Abadi said we will not send the Iraqi Army deep into the Sunni province. Again, we will get a national guard.

Senator JOHNSON. Okay. I have got a lot more questions, but I am out of time. So thank you.

The CHAIRMAN. Senator McCain.

Senator MCCAIN. I thank the witnesses, and I thank you, Mr. Connable, for being here. And, Ambassador Ford, thank you for your outstanding service. Mr. Connable, if I have got you right, the Iranians are in a position of significant influence in Baghdad right now, is that correct?

Mr. CONNABLE. I believe that to be true.

Senator MCCAIN. That cannot be good for our interests over time.

Mr. CONNABLE. I agree with you.

Senator MCCAIN. And another legacy of total withdrawal.

Mr. CONNABLE. I think that would have happened anyway. I think it was exacerbated by the fact that the western and northern parts of Iraq collapsed. I cannot attribute it directly to our withdrawal.

Senator MCCAIN. Ambassador Ford, is there any doubt about the viability if given the proper training and equipment, and you mentioned—my understanding is that ISIS has given them as much as $2,000 a month because they have got plenty of money; that there is no doubt in your mind about if we do it right, that the FSA is viable.

Ambassador FORD. With much less support than what we have been giving, they have actually held ground and advanced in a few places.

Senator MCCAIN. And I share that view, and the thing that is frustrating to me sometimes is all of this stuff that people accept—they have made a deal with ISIS, they cannot fight. And having known them, as you have known them a lot better than I do, they will fight, and they need our support in order to do that successfully. But they are not about to become part of ISIS or even al-Nusra if from time to time they have to cooperation because of their straightened circumstances.

Ambassador FORD. That is absolutely true that they are in a tough situation. A two-front war is never fun. But I am very impressed that they have held up as well as they have despite the difficult circumstances.

Senator MCCAIN. So in my view, I conclude that it is an excuse that people use, frankly, to not have us involved. And I do not expect you to comment on that, but here we are. Again, I want to sort of pursue what I was pursuing—a line that I was—with Secretary Kerry. We are going to train them. We are going to equip them. But we are not going to protect them from these airstrikes that are so devastating to their capability—the barrel bombs, the helicopters, the fixed wing, which, by the way, as you know, is the main way for Bashir al-Assad to move his people and material around Iraq.

So is it not—we are asking them to fight. We are asking them to risk their lives, and yet we will not give them the protection from the air attacks, which would be the major source of casualties for them. Make sense of that for me.

Ambassador FORD. Well, I think we both know that there are concerns that if we provide surface-to-air missiles, that they will be somehow transferred to the Nusra front or to ISIL or something like that. One encouraging sign I take from the recent fighting, Senator McCain, up in Hama, which is a city between Damascus and Aleppo, the regime has a very important air base. And using stand-off weapons, mortars and such things, the Free Syrian Army was actually able to bring most of the air traffic at the Hama military airport to a stop.

Senator MCCAIN. I am impressed with what they do, but if I am a Syrian and I am being armed and trained and asked to go into battle, and I see that we are not giving us the capability even, much less the United States taking out that air power, it is not great for my morale.

Ambassador FORD. Our refusal to provide surface-to-air missiles has been a gigantic irritant not only to the armed opposition fighters, but to the population in generation that is getting barrel bombed. There is no doubt of that.

Senator MCCAIN. Did you see—I am sure you saw the quote I gave from Secretary Gates, his comment today that we really cannot succeed without boots on the ground is basically what he was saying.

Ambassador FORD. I did not see Secretary Gates' remarks.

Senator MCCAIN. Well, I guess I could read it to you again, but do you think that in your estimate that the 5,000 being trained and not taking out Bashir al-Assad's air assets, telling everybody that it is ISIL as if we cannot address two adversaries at the same time, that the chances of success without much more significant involvement on the ground, and it does not mean combat units, but forward air controllers, special forces, et cetera, that we are going to have to—basically Secretary Gates was saying we are going to have to do that over time.

Ambassador FORD. I think several things on this, Senator McCain. First, 5,000 is obviously not enough. Syria is a really big country. But I think there is going to be more than 5,000. And I think already elements of the armed opposition, excluding Nusra and ISIL, 80,000 plus. The 5,000 might be one of the better parts, and it might be the part that we would have more influence with. But frankly, we will have more influence if we provide more weapons and cash anyway.

Second point, with respect to ISIL first or not, I just think realistically, of course, the armed opposition is going to fight Assad even as they fight the Islamic State. We would be foolish to think otherwise. So——

Senator MCCAIN. The question is, Do we help them to do that?

Ambassador FORD. Well, I think we——

Senator MCCAIN. The way we help them to do that is you neutralize the air assets.

Ambassador FORD. Yes. But we have not neutralized the air assets obviously, and there have been horrific barrel bombs attacks almost daily. We have been providing other help. We suffer credibility problems, Senator McCain. I am not going to argue with you on that.

We have been providing other help, which they use against the regime. I would actually argue that help that we have provided has actually enabled them to make advances in places like southern Syria and northern Syria. And the aid has actually been effective that way.

Senator MCCAIN. And there is no doubt in your mind they are not going to join forces with any extremist organization.

Ambassador FORD. As I mentioned—I am glad you asked that question. I actually have raised with them when I was working at the State Department the problem that Nusra poses for us, and I get a very consistent answer. I got a very consistent answer, which is we do not like them either. We do not like al-Qaeda. Now, these are defected army officers or, you know, people who were civilians, but were high up in the Syrian military before they went into civilian life, and then they became leaders in the Free Syrian Army.

They say, we do not like them either, but you cannot ask us to not deal with them when they are over in the next neighborhood, and we are pushing against the regime, and they are pushing, and not coordinate with them. They said, that is not reasonable because we do not have enough stuff to do this by ourselves. And they were very blunt with it. They said, you give us more stuff, we will not have to deal with them.

Senator MCCAIN. Mr. Connable, do you have a comment on that aspect of it?

Mr. CONNABLE. In regards to Syrian air power, I think it would be very interesting to see if we eventually do put Title 10 advisors on the ground on Syria, what effect that will have on the Assad regime's decision on whether or not to attack the Syrian opposition. So if our special forces teams are providing higher level advice there, I think the Syrian Government will be very reluctant to attack those forces.

Senator MCCAIN. Thank you very much.

The CHAIRMAN. Thank you, Senator. One last question, Mr. Connable. You made a very pointed effort to make the case that it was the Sunni awakening that was the critical element in the success. Yes, the surge. Yes, the other elements. But that without the Sunni awakening, we might not have had the success that we ultimately achieve there.

So what steps must, in your view, the Iraqi Government take to facilitate reconciliation with the alienated Sunni tribes in Anbar province and other Sunni majority areas in order to reduce political support for ISIL and to get them to have a second awakening?

Mr. CONNABLE. Yes. As I have stated, Mr. Chairman, that is the fundamental question. There is one major problem and, I think, one major opportunity. The major problem is the Sunni polity and the political leadership are so badly fragmented, that there is really no hope for some kind of negotiated settlement at the top level or even with regional leaders. There simply is not enough credibility there in the Sunni leadership to allow that to happen.

However, the real opportunity is that the Sunni, in a very kind of dispersed way, have very clearly enumerated a lot of the grievances that they think are most critical to them, and it is almost like a laundry list. I listed a few of them in my—in my written testimony.

But I think the good news here is that Prime Minister al-Abadi also listed another laundry list of these when he assumed office and put his government together, and that was a very positive step. So he has already announced the things that need to be done. The trick is executing. And I think about 50 percent of the things that he identified, and you could probably add in another small group of things that would be really critical, he could probably do with the stroke of a pen. The others would require deliberation of the government.

I think he should do whatever he can under his own authority immediately and together. If he is able to do that, then Sunni that I have spoken to, I think, would react quite favorably to that. It is a first step, but it is an important one.

The CHAIRMAN. So even though the Sunni leadership, as you described it, is fragmented, there are some universal issues that they have raised that if addressed as part of reconciliation would be cross-cutting.

Mr. CONNABLE. I think Prime Minister al-Abadi is speaking to the Sunni people, not to Sunni leaders. I think they are cross-cutting, yes.

The CHAIRMAN. Well, this has been very helpful. You have the thanks of the committee for your insights.

This record will remain open until the close of business on Friday.

And with that, this hearing is adjourned.

[Whereupon, at 6:40 p.m., the hearing was adjourned.]

———————

ADDITIONAL MATERIAL SUBMITTED FOR THE RECORD

RESPONSES OF SECRETARY JOHN F. KERRY TO QUESTIONS SUBMITTED BY SENATOR MARCO RUBIO

Question. On Iran.—Secretary Kerry, several days ago, you indicated that the United States might be open to including Iran in the coalition being organized to challenge ISIL.

◆ Have there been any conversations with Iranian officials regarding potential co-operation against ISIL?

Answer. If we believe that it would be useful to discuss counter-ISIL efforts with Iran, we may do that on the margins of the P5+1 talks, as we have done in the past. We are open to engagement with Iranian officials in specific circumstances when doing so could help to advance U.S. interests. But let me be clear that the nuclear negotiation is a separate issue from actions regarding ISIL.

◆ Would you describe Iran as a state that furthers or undermines regional stability?

Answer. While Iran has, in common with the emerging international consensus, a strong interest in seeing ISIL defeated, we remain deeply concerned about many aspects of Iran's foreign policy in the region. In particular, we continue to express our concerns about Iran's destabilizing activities in Syria where it, along with Lebanese Hezbollah (LH), continues to support the Assad regime by providing weapons, training, and material assistance to Assad's forces.

◆ Under what scenarios would the Obama administration cooperate with Iran against ISIL?

Answer. As previously mentioned, if and when there are specific circumstances in which engagement with Iran would advance our interests in countering ISIL, we are open to such engagement. However, let me be clear that the United States will not coordinate military action with Iran.

◆ As military actions against ISIL expand, what actions will the United States take to avoid implicitly supporting Iranian or Syrian forces currently combating ISIL?

Answer. We are not coordinating with the Assad regime or Iran regarding any planning that the U.S. military is developing. The President has emphasized repeatedly that Bashar al-Assad has lost legitimacy in Syria and should go. Supporting the moderate opposition will support our goal of degrading and destroying ISIL and our goal of pressuring Assad to accept a negotiated political settlement. As we've made very clear, the United States will take lawful action when our people are threatened, regardless of geographic boundaries.

Question. On the Strategy.—The President compared his strategy to confront ISIL to very limited counterterror operations carried out in Yemen and Somalia.

◆ Are Yemen and Somalia today the model of stability the President seeks to achieve in Iraq?

◆ Is the threat posed by ISIL in the territories it controls in Iraq and Syria comparable to that of al-Shabab in Somalia or AQ in the Arabian Peninsula in Yemen?

Answer. The U.S. strategy to defeat the Islamic State of Iraq and the Levant (ISIL) involves five interdependent lines of effort: (1) providing military support to the Iraqi Security Forces (ISF) and to the moderate Syrian opposition; (2) cutting off the flow of foreign terrorist fighters to ISIL; (3) countering ISIL's financing and funding; (4) addressing humanitarian crises; and (5) de-legitimizing ISIL's ideology. Simultaneously, we will support the efforts of the Government of Iraq to govern inclusively. This is a broad strategy, which builds on the model the President announced at the National Defense University and at West Point, with many elements that will require a long-term commitment to achieve success. We are not indicating that the threats emanating from Somalia and Yemen are entirely parallel to those of Iraq and Syria, nor are we holding up Yemen and Somalia as our end-state goal for Iraq and Syria in years to come. Rather, the administration has pointed to these lines of effort as examples of where the United States has used a comprehensive strategy and had seen some successes.

In Yemen and Somalia, the United States has taken steps to build up the capacity of forces on the ground to take the fight to terrorists in their own country, and we have used our military and intelligence capabilities to support the efforts of those indigenous forces. With our support, al-Shabaab has been pushed out of nearly all major urban areas in Somalia by local Somali forces and the African Union Mission in Somalia (AMISOM). Across the country, Somalis have chosen peace, local governance, and a national identity instead of al-Shabaab. In April and May, the Yemeni military conducted an offensive that drove Al Qaeda in the Arabian Peninsula (AQAP) from its safe havens in Abyan and Shabwah governorates. While AQAP remains a lethal threat, it no longer openly controls large swaths of territory.

Beyond our military and intelligence activities, the administration has also worked with partners inside and outside these regions and even in the United States to prevent the flow of foreign terrorist fighters to Yemen and Somalia. The U.S. Government has used its financial tools and mobilized international efforts to cut off external contributions to AQAP and al-Shabaab. We have provided alternative messages to their hateful propaganda. Our counterterrorism efforts in both countries have been underpinned by a comprehensive strategy to support the government and the people as they pursue challenging but important reforms through their political transition processes, recognizing that stability and security also depend on continued political, economic, and humanitarian progress. While severe challenges remain in both countries, we strongly believe that our counterterrorism efforts will only succeed in the context of broader political and economic advancement.

Using this model in Yemen and Somalia, we have been able to contain the threat to the U.S. homeland, degrade those terrorist-affiliated organizations, and in some instances, eliminated their top leadership. Like these efforts, the fight against ISIL will be waged through a steady, relentless effort to take out ISIL wherever it exists, using our air power, support from a growing coalition of foreign partners, and our support for partner forces on the ground, complemented by a broader campaign that brings all elements of national power to bear in countering this threat.

Question. Former U.S. Ambassador to Syria, Robert Ford, said in June: "We need, and we have long needed, to help moderates in the Syrian opposition with both weapons and other nonlethal assistance. Had we done that a couple of years ago, had we ramped it up, frankly, the al-Qaeda groups that have been winning adherents would have been unable to comply with the moderates."

- ◆ Do you agree with Ambassador Ford that the failure to provide lethal and nonlethal assistance to the mainstream Syrian opposition helped give rise to ISIS and other jihadist groups?
- ◆ Wouldn't we have better options before us now if he had taken that route early on?

Answer. We have been providing nonlethal assistance to the moderate opposition since 2013; with the rise of ISIL, we are increasing nonlethal assistance as well as moving forward with the train and equip program, along with our regional partners. The moderate opposition is being squeezed from both sides, forced to confront ISIL, other extremists, and the Assad regime. In order to degrade and ultimately defeat ISIL, as well as to counter the Assad regime, we need to strengthen the moderate opposition, and will do so with a joint State Department and DOD train and equip program as authorized by Congress. With this new effort, we'll provide training and equipment to help the moderate opposition grow stronger and take on ISIL terrorists inside Syria. This program will be hosted outside of Syria, in partnership with allies, and it will be matched by our increasing support for Iraqi Government and Kurdish Forces in Iraq.

Question. A month ago, the President referred to the moderate Syrian opposition as "former doctors, farmers, pharmacists, and so forth." He went on to say "There's not as much capacity as you would hope."

- ◆ Can you describe what changed the President's assessment of the opposition since then to such an extent that he now hopes to provide them lethal assistance?
- ◆ What percentage of the opposition in Syria is made up of extremist or terrorist elements and what percentage would you deem moderates that we can work with?
- ◆ Is it still possible for the non-jihadist rebels to topple Assad and gain control of the entire country? In essence, will they be able to not just take over Damas-

cus, but also drive the jihadists out of northern Syria? If it is, what will it take for that to happen?

Answer. As the President said in his ''60 Minutes'' interview that was broadcast on September 28: ''Keep in mind my statement referred to the outlook 2 years ago. The point that I made then, which is absolutely true, is that for us to just start arming inexperienced fighters who we hadn't vetted would leave us in a situation where we didn't know and couldn't sort out who was a potential ISIL or al-Nusra member and who was somebody that we could work with. For us to just go blind on that would have been counterproductive and would not have helped the situation.''

The Free Syrian Army (FSA) is a term to describe various armed groups that share the goal of overthrowing the Assad regime, and includes secularists as well as moderate Islamist fighting groups. The FSA has proven its will and ability to stand up against ISIL, at the same time Assad's air force was attacking them with ground forces and barrel bombs.

Estimates of the total number of violent extremist fighters or the moderate opposition are complex, and the most detailed estimates are based on sensitive information. The most recent relevant analysis of ISIL is that it has between 20,000 and 31,000 fighters. By way of comparison, estimates of the moderate opposition are larger: tens of thousands of nationalist Syrian fighters committed to facing ISIL are present today in Aleppo, Idlib, Deir al-Zor, and Daraa.

The United States is already supporting some of these fighters with nonlethal assistance, but the train and equip program will enable us to increase our support. It could also help deter ISIL recruitment efforts as the moderate opposition demonstrates greater support from abroad. Together with our partners, the United States is supporting the Syrian opposition to be a counterweight to the terrorists of ISIL and the brutality of the Assad regime.

Question. What role is Qatar playing in our coalition against ISIL? How do you respond to concerns that Qatar is playing a double game, trying to work with the United States, while simultaneously retaining ties to terrorist groups inside of Syria?

Answer. Qatar is an important partner in the coalition to degrade and defeat the Islamic State of Iraq and the Levant (ISIL). As a signatory to the Jeddah Communique, Qatar joined a host of countries in the region and the United States in pledging to support a comprehensive strategy to fight ISIL. Qatar has been outspoken in its condemnations of ISIL, with Minister of Foreign Affairs Dr. Khalid bin Mohammed Al Attiyah stating that he is ''repelled by their [ISIL's] views, their violent methods, and their ambitions.'' The Qatari Ministry of Foreign Affairs has also issued statements congratulating the new Iraqi Prime Minister Haidar al-Abadi on his appointment and welcoming the formation of a new Iraqi Government, helping to establish the regional legitimacy of the fledgling government.

Qatar joined the United States in initiating airstrikes in Syria, and hosts the al-Udeid Air Base, a critical military facility for the coalition's air campaign against ISIL. We continue to work closely with Qatar on other issues related to terrorism, including efforts to combat contributions from private citizens in the region to violent extremist groups. On September 16, Qatar announced a new law regulating charities that, if fully implemented and deployed, will be an important step in its progress in cracking down on terror financing.

Question. Press reports indicate that ISIL receives significant funding from cross-border smuggling of oil into Turkey. Many foreign jihadists that have joined ISIL's ranks also have transited through Turkey on their way to Syria.

♦ How would you characterize your discussions with Turkey about both of these challenges? Is the Turkish Government doing enough to address both of these issues?

Answer. We have raised with Turkish officials at the highest level our serious concerns regarding ISIL financing via black market oil sales and smuggling in the region. While Turkish officials have already taken some action to curb oil smuggling, they realize more needs to be done and have promised to take additional steps, including bolstering the Customs Ministry's role in antismuggling efforts. U.S. and Turkish agencies have also stepped up the exchange of analysis and intelligence on oil smuggling and other ISIL financial activity to assist Turkey in taking more effective action.

Similarly, we are working closely with Turkey and other European partners to stem the flow of foreign fighters into Syria. Turkish Government leaders acknowledge that the extremist presence in Syria poses a threat to Turkey, the region, and the home countries of foreign fighters. Turkey faces particular challenges given its geographical location and the high volume of legitimate travelers. As the conflict in Syria has continued, the threat posed by violent extremist elements has prompted stronger action by the Turkish Government to counter foreign fighter travel across its borders. For example, the Turkish Government is working to tighten entry and exit controls.

We have an ongoing, robust dialogue with Turkey on ways to improve our counterterrorism cooperation, including better information-sharing, curbing of terrorism finance more effectively, and stronger border security. Special Presidential Envoy for the Global Coalition to Counter ISIL John Allen traveled to Turkey October 8–10 to discuss coalition efforts to degrade and defeat ISIL through a variety of means, including efforts to stop terrorist financing and countering the flow of foreign fighters.

RESPONSES OF SECRETARY JOHN KERRY TO QUESTIONS SUBMITTED BY SENATOR TOM UDALL

Question. How much has food insecurity contributed to ISIS' rise, and what is the international community and USAID doing to help ensure that access to food is protected among refugees, displaced populations, and even the Iraqi military?

Answer. ISIL has preyed upon grievances and vulnerabilities within Syrian communities. We have not been tracking food insecurity specifically, but needs continue to expand. The international humanitarian community, with the U.S. Government as the largest donor, continues to feed millions of Syrians every month, both inside the country and in neighboring countries. In August, the U.N. World Food Programme (WFP), USAID's primary partner in the region, delivered food assistance to more than 4.1 million people inside Syria in August—the largest number of people reached in 1 month since the conflict began. Distributions by WFP were taking place in areas that ISIS has since conquered, and WFP can now no longer access these areas. Gathering the necessary public health data to assess acute malnutrition rates in a war zone is difficult. Comprehensive food security and nutrition surveys have not been possible since 2010 due to the conflict, but there have not been reports of the emergency-level acute malnutrition rates that would indicate severe food insecurity inside Syria during the conflict. While food prices in Syria have risen dramatically, Syria had better-than-expected harvests in 2012 and 2013 despite the conflict; those harvests, along with international food assistance, helped offset what would otherwise have been a more severe decline in food security due to the war.

USAID-funded food assistance to internally displaced and conflict-affected Syrians inside the country and to Syrian refugees in neighboring countries is very carefully targeted and distributed to ensure that it reaches only intended beneficiaries and is not used for nonhumanitarian purposes. Inside Syria, USAID-funded WFP food parcels reach specific, vulnerable communities, and our NGO partners deliver food parcels directly to beneficiary households and provide flour to bakeries that benefit affected communities. In neighboring countries, WFP provides USAID-funded food assistance to Syrian refugees in strict accordance with refugee registration lists; assistance is provided either via voucher, for which refugees must prove their identity, or via food distribution to specific households.

In Iraq, the Public Distribution Systems (PDS), managed by the Iraqi Government, used to provide basic food rations to nearly all food-insecure Iraqi families on a regular basis, including in areas that ISIS now controls. In those areas PDS has now been suspended. We have not heard any reports of the excessively high food prices in Iraq, or of the emergency-level acute malnutrition rates. Malnutrition rates are generally very low in Iraq and there are no indications that this has changed recently or that food insecurity has led to increased support for ISIS. The food security situation has been stable in recent years and USAID had not needed to contribute food assistance since 2008.

Due to a generous contribution from Saudi Arabia, WFP's emergency food operations in Iraq are covered through December. Ensuring food assistance reaches those in need remains a priority, and WFP has consistently increased the geographic and numeric reach of its operations since conflict intensified in June. USAID will consider support for WFP in coming months as necessary based on review of WFP's pipeline and assessment of need.

USAID does not provide food assistance to the Iraqi military or indeed to any military.

Question. The conflict in Syria has continued for over 3 years and taken nearly 200,000 lives. If ISIS is beaten back in Syria but the underlying conditions of the Syrian civil war remain, should we expect another radical Islamic group to emerge?

Answer. We have long been working to lay the basis for effective peace negotiations and a post-Asasd Syrian government. Our ongoing support to local communities, together with the political leadership of the opposition help opposition-held areas effectively govern, rebuild, and establish law and order. This is why we continue to support the local councils, civil defense brigades, and teachers in opposition-held areas. The moderate opposition is already benefiting from this help as it administers areas in Aleppo, Hama, Northern Lattakia, Idlib, Daraa, and some areas around Damascus, while building credibility with citizens of their communities. While no plan is risk-proof, our goal is to empower civilian institutions, together with vetted brigades on the ground, in partnership with local communities we support, to fill in any space that is vacated by ISIL.

Supporting the moderate opposition is essential to our political strategy. There is no military solution to the conflict. Increasing support to the moderate opposition can put pressure on the regime and promote more conducive conditions for a negotiated political settlement. The regime has created the present instability and the conditions for the growth of violent extremism among an otherwise nonextremist population.

The administration has built an international coalition against ISIL working across multiple lines of effort. In coordination with our international partners, we will also redouble efforts to cut off funding flows to ISIL; enhance intelligence collection on ISIL; counter the group's violent, extremist ideology; and stem the flow of foreign fighters into the area. Additionally, the President committed to working with our international partners to continue providing humanitarian assistance to innocent civilians who have been displaced, to stabilize a potentially vulnerable population. The United States will also continue to work to help prevent mass atrocities, particularly against vulnerable religious and ethnic minorities, since these can also be destabilizing and lead to a cycle of violence.

Question. One year ago many of us were concerned about plans to arm these so-called Syrian moderates because weapons could get in the hands of al-Nusra, which is a powerful rebel group allied with al-Qaeda. Who is backing al-Nusra in the region and what is the administration's strategy for dealing with them should ISIS be degraded and destroyed?

Answer. The support structure of violent extremist organizations is complex and diverse. Al-Nusra Front, which is a mix of foreign fighters and Syrian nationals, like ISIL, has received its financial support from criminal activities, abuse of nonprofit organizations, looting of cultural heritage sites, and some external support. The recent legislation authorizing the train-and-equip program requires us to vet out, at a minimum, those associated with terrorist groups, including, but not limited to, ISIL, al-Nusra Front, Ahrar al-Sham and other al-Qaeda related groups, and Hezbollah.

Question a,b,c. If we look around the Middle East, there are radical Islamic elements in many nations that have lost central government control. We have been fighting the Taliban for over a decade, long after driving them from power and eliminating the senior al-Qaeda leaders responsible for 9/11. Libya is in a civil war. Iraq is in a civil and sectarian war. Similar situations persist in Yemen and Somalia and Sudan. Syria is perhaps the worst example. We seem to be engaging in many of these conflicts in one way or another.

♦ With our engagement in each of these areas, are we focusing on individuals and groups that are seeking to attack American interests and our homeland?

Answer (a). The Taliban (Afghanistan).—The President has been clear that while our combat mission will be over by the end of the year, we will continue to pursue our objective in Afghanistan of disrupting threats posed by al-Qaeda. We will advance that objective with a twofold mission of supporting counterterrorism operations against the remnants of al-Qaeda as well as a broader effort to train and equip Afghan Forces to ensure that Afghanistan does not again become a safe haven for al-Qaeda and other extremist groups.

Answer (b). Somalia.—The United States has designated the Somalia-based group al-Shabaab a terrorist organization. Al-Shabaab's leaders have publicly pledged allegiance with al-Qaeda and have called for attacks against the United States and U.S. citizens abroad. The group leverages its regional network to conduct terrorist operations.

U.S. counterterrorism programs are aligned with strategic regional priorities to assist Somalia's efforts in monitoring and securing its own borders, detecting and disrupting terrorist plots, and investigating terrorist incidents. We have funded programs to build capacity in law enforcement, crisis response, border security, and strengthening the rule of law.

The Federal Government of Somalia works in partnership with the United States and other regional partners to deny and disrupt al-Shabaab operations within Somalia. We have also conducted unilateral strikes against targets, including against former al-Shabaab emir Ahmed Abdi "Godane." A key focus of our engagement is to strengthen the Somali Government's capacity to provide sustainable security that will eliminate al-Shabaab's ability to regroup and regain footholds in Somalia.

Answer (c). Syria.—Yes, that is always the primary concern. For example, that is why in Syria we have been tracking for several years the al-Nusra Front and the "Khorasan Group," a term sometimes used to refer to a network of al-Nusra Front and al-Qaeda core terrorists who share a history of training operatives, facilitating fighters and money, and planning attacks against U.S. and Western targets. These operatives are seasoned and very dangerous individuals who have fought and lived together in Chechnya, Afghanistan, Pakistan, Iraq, Iran, Yemen, and North Africa. They have many years, if not decades, of experience conducting and planning attacks against innocents, and they have brought advanced skill sets to Syria.

ISIL also poses a threat to the people of Iraq and Syria, and the broader Middle East—including American citizens, personnel and facilities. If left unchecked, these terrorists could pose a growing threat beyond that region, including to the United States. While we have not yet detected specific plotting against our homeland, ISIL leaders have threatened America and our allies. Our Intelligence Community believes that thousands of foreigners—including Europeans and some Americans—have joined them in Syria and Iraq. Trained and battle-hardened, these fighters could try to return to their home countries and carry out deadly attacks.

Success for us is working to methodically target such organizations, their external plotters, and operatives to prevent attacks as best we can, particularly any plotting against U.S. interests or the homeland, and to set the conditions in place so that these groups are defeated in the long run. This will have to be done in concert with partners on the ground.